# NATURAL HISTORY
*of the*
# INTELLECT

# Natural History

## of the

# INTELLECT

The Last Lectures of
*Ralph Waldo Emerson*

EDITED BY
MAURICE YORK & RICK SPAULDING

WRIGHTWOOD

P R E S S

Wrightwood Press
PO Box 14702, Chicago, IL 60614-0702
www.wrightwoodpress.org

The lectures printed in this volume are reprinted by permission
of the Ralph Waldo Emerson Memorial Association
and by permission of Houghton Library, Harvard University
from manuscripts in the Ralph Waldo Emerson papers:
Harvard Lectures, 1870-1871, bMS Am 1280.212 (1-19)
Poetry and Imagination: Morals, bMS Am 1280.214 (4)
Detailed editorial documentation and commentary
on the lectures can be found in
*Natural History of the Intellect: Emerson's Cambridge Course of 1871, a Critical Edition*
forthcoming from the Wrightwood Press.

Cover montage images: [Columbia River Oregon, Showing Crown Poitn and Vista House],
courtesy of the Library of Congress Prints and Photographs Division.
Star cluster NGC 602 in the Small Magellenic Cloud, courtesy of STScl and NASA.

NON-PROFITS, LIBRARIES, EDUCATIONAL INSTITUTIONS,
WORKSHOP SPONSORS, STUDY GROUPS, ETC.
Special discounts and bulk purchases are available.
Please email sales@wrightwoodpress.org for more information.
You are welcome to reproduce and use any part of this work, up to 25%,
for non-profit personal or group study in print or electronic form,
including electronic reserves. For inquiries about
use in excess of 25%, or for commercial use or re-publication,
please email permissions@wrightwoodpress.org

ISBN 978-0-9801190-1-5

Yet I see that Intellect is a science of degrees, and that, as man is conscious of the law of vegetable and animal nature, so he is aware of an Intellect which overhangs his consciousness like a sky, of degree above degree, and heaven within heaven. In its last aspect, it is the supreme fact we know, is the commander of matter, and is the life and order by which matter exists.

—*Ralph Waldo Emerson*

# Contents

❧

# PREFACE

~

ON A CLEAR FRIDAY IN APRIL, 1871, RALPH WALDO EMERSON stood before a class of students in a hall at Harvard University to deliver the final lecture of his "Cambridge Course." At seventeen lectures, the series—which he gave under the working title of the "Natural History of the Intellect"—was the longest sustained speaking engagement of his career and the most complex thematic material he had attempted to deliver in a public forum. At a pace of two lectures a week requiring him to travel by train from Concord to Cambridge from February through April, the schedule was more reasonable than the three a week he had given the previous spring. For a man supposedly entering the twilight of his career, Emerson showed remarkable perseverance in the undertaking. For two and a half months he had made his best effort towards condensing, summarizing, and putting forward what he considered to be his best thoughts of more than three decades,—an army, as he described it, of 10,000 days that he had marshaled to his side. Yet in the final weeks of the course he had become exhausted, even dis-

heartened with the exertion and his performance. He had cut short
the series and compressed the final three lectures into a single week
so that he could take, at his family's behest, a much needed vaca-
tion and journey westward. On April 10th he left for California by
way of Pullman car. He had completed the last significant lectures
of his forty-five year career.

By the time he delivered the Cambridge Course, Emerson's
seven volumes of essays and two books of poetry, in addition to
hundreds upon hundreds of lectures given to audiences from
Maine to California, had made him one of the most well-known
and beloved men of letters of his time. His profound influence on
writers such as Hawthorne, Melville, Whitman, and Dickinson
earned him the title, among later generations, of the Father of
American culture. The clear prose and high idealism of Emerson's
published essays—*Nature*, "Self-Reliance," "The American Scholar,"
"The Poet"—have inspired an audience that spans the globe, and
his aphorisms and metaphors have become inextricably woven into
the deep vernacular of American culture. Yet the greater part of
Emerson's lasting fame, the bedrock of his world-historic place in
the progress of thought and letters, rests on the events and prod-
ucts of his middle years. High school students will recite his place
as the figurehead of the Transcendentalists, know about the book
*Nature* and the "all-seeing eyeball", and indicate that he was a good
friend of Thoreau—all things that were true of Emerson in his thir-
ties and early forties. The genuine measure of his life—his mission,
if one could name it so—would seem logically identified with the

better part of his work that has had an enduring impact.

In his *Memoir of Ralph Waldo Emerson*, published shortly after Emerson's death, James Elliot Cabot wrote that the man who had become known as the Sage of Concord appeared to have regarded the "Natural History of the Intellect" as the "chief task of his life." At the time Cabot wrote this statement, the lectures were unpublished in any form and completely unknown to any but the students who had heard Emerson deliver them over a decade earlier. The Memoir made the claim with little elaboration or explanation before moving on to later events. At best, it seemed an odd assertion to put forward. Yet Cabot, a close friend of Emerson's and personally selected by him to be executor of his literary estate, held in his hands the weight of evidence to make an assessment as consequential as the question of a life task. For over a decade, beginning while Emerson was still alive and continuing after his death in 1882, Cabot had immersed himself in the essayist and lecturer's voluminous output of journals, notebooks, lectures, diaries, letters, and miscellaneous papers. At the time he wrote the *Memoir*, he knew Emerson's mind perhaps better than anyone—knew it so well that he had taken it upon himself to draw together unpublished passages that he mined from Emerson's papers and arrange them as complete essays to be published, with the family's approval, under Emerson's own name. Cabot, the close friend and competent editor, easily recognized the importance that Emerson himself placed on the Natural History project, yet Cabot, the metaphysician and trained philosopher, saw little more than gestures and indications of what he thought Emerson was hinting at—a reaction against systematic reasoning in favor of momentary impressions that, in Cabot's estimation, philosophically "empties out the child with the bath." After surveying a lifetime of accumulated writing, Cabot concluded that there was little "new" to be found in the lectures, at least nothing that "disclosed any novelty of method" that would merit publication.

Despite Cabot's qualitative conclusion about the worth of the 1870-71 lectures to the canon of Emerson's work, his indication that Emerson considered the project to be the leading purpose of his life gave the hint of a compelling story well worth exploring. The first stirrings of what would become the "Natural History" had appeared thirty-three years earlier in Emerson's journal for 1837, as he was preparing the lecture that launched his career—"The American Scholar." The oration would be his thunder clap to shake the drowsy, imitative drone of American culture and academics, a rousing exploration of the major influences and trials that define the path of self-development for the modern student who would understand the times he lives in and his own place in them. Even greater than the question of self-knowledge was the mystery of what was larger than the self, the tide of thought and striving that seemed to roll through successive generations, scattered in the witnesses it found in poets, artists, philosophers, and kings. Emerson's germinal idea was that the omnipresent spiritual forces that stand just beyond the reach of our physical senses should be just as understandable as the natural world visible to our every day sight—that the study of spiritual laws should unveil the history of the mind as surely as the study of natural laws reveals the history of the earth. By December of 1837, he elaborated what he meant by a "history of the mind," showing it as the action of the Intellect in human history, its outpouring in the great cultures—the Persian, the Egyptian, the Greek—and reappearance in the modern day. The concept grew and spread its roots for almost a year. In April of 1838, Emerson gave himself an imperative—"Write the Natural History of Reason."

That May Emerson turned thirty-five. While not fully matured, his habit of thought was fairly well established when he set himself this task. His first impression of a thought or idea, his initial attempt to capture and flesh it out, was generally set down in his journal as part of his daily writing, often accompanied by quotations or anecdotes from reading and conversation. The best of these thoughts he would pull out and group together as subject matter for a lecture, finding a common theme or thread and then lending structure to the whole by outline and arrangement, many times approaching the same concept from different points of view through repeated lectures in order to hone it down to its core components, its essential truth. The lectures themselves became source material for essays, a new and more advanced stage of writing in which the discoveries of the lectures were again recombined, arranged, augmented, and set down in carefully formulated language. Emerson's process was iterative and didactic, building up, tearing down, re-forming and arranging thoughts over the course of months, often years, before he was satisfied that he could set them down in published form. It was the entirety of this process in all of its successive stages that Emerson was committing to in giving himself the task of writing the Natural History of Reason. The enormity of the project proved to be greater than he could have imagined on that spring day in 1838.

Emerson's first full exposition of the subject, appropriately entitled "Intellect," appeared in printed form at the height of the Transcendental Movement in his first book of Essays (1841). The essay—one of the shorter pieces in the volume—was in essence an extended definition, an initial effort to lay the groundwork for the expansive project by outlining its central concept. "Intellect is the simple power anterior to all action or construction," he wrote in the opening paragraph. "Gladly would I unfold in calm degrees a natural history of the intellect, but what man has yet been able to mark the steps and boundaries of that transparent essence?" The short years that followed saw the waning of the Transcendental Movement and the breaking up, in 1845, of the Concord Circle, as his friends were known. The inspiration that had once enlivened Emerson's journals and lectures seemed to retreat along with the spirit of cultural and social reform. He felt in his work a gloominess that matched the dusty cloud kicked up by the political maneuvering that marked the prelude to the Mexican War.

An escape to England in 1848—his second trip across the sea—brought him within the grasp of that inspiration once again. During his stay in London he returned to the theme of the Intellect and wrote three lectures under the title of "Mind and Manners in the Nineteenth Century." The lectures proposed a kind of science of the Intellect, a study of the laws of thought. Finding much in the new work to elaborate and pursue, he repeated the series three times over the course of the next two years. Yet the renewed inspiration visible in the lectures battled with a feeling of ennui that had beset him on the voyage back to America. Over the next decade he pursued a frustrating search for "a whip for my top" that continued against the backdrop of the gathering storm of the Civil War. The "Natural History" project recurred to him from time to time, particularly after meeting the poet Walt Whitman for the first time in 1855, but always in the background, in the privacy of his journals. Early in 1858, having collected for two and a half years "a goodly quantity of material that ought to interest goodly heads," Emerson approached the topic of the Intellect for a third time and from a wholly new perspective. This fresh delivery of the series in two different venues gave him great satisfaction.

A natural question arises about Emerson's motivation for pursuing the Natural History project to such great lengths: what drove him to return to it time and time again, never quite satisfied with what had come before, always with a fresh sense that some new territory remained to explore? The many threads of the project are deeply tied to Emerson's own life and personal development. One might say that Emerson's character is at the very core of the *Natural History*, just as Thoreau's character formed the heart of *Walden* and as Whitman's did *Leaves of Grass*. Emerson held one goal for himself as a lecturer: to inspire the individuals that had come to hear him and awaken them to their own potential, to their origin in spirit and the wisdom in nature presented to them every day as a picture of the human being in its divine proportion. He sought to be a teacher of the spirit to his countrymen, to speak with such force to "get the soul out of bed, out of her deep habitual sleep, out into God's universe, to a perception of its beauty and hearing of its call, and your vulgar man, your prosy, selfish sensualist awakes, a god, and is conscious of force to shake the world." In essence, the Natural History project had started to take shape,— slowly, surely, largely in the background of his more public work,—as the visible realization of that goal. Particularly with the second iteration of the lectures in 1858, he had begun to lay the foundations of the project as a path—a suggestion how, in a materialistic age when the spirit is hidden and obscured from first-hand experience, to recognize the activity of the Intellect in the world around us, respond to the ethical duty that such recognition lays upon the conscience, and begin to develop higher powers of perception. For the interested reader, the editors' biography, *Ralph Waldo Emerson: the Infinitude of the Private Man*, explores Emerson's self-development and character, and their relation to his lectures and written works, including the *Natural History*.

Following the great conflagration of the Civil War, Emerson returned to the Natural History project once more with new commitment, reworking and expanding the thoughts yet again. In 1866 he presented six lectures that emphasized a new theme: the activity of the Intellect in history and the significance to modern life of the presence of the Intellect. His new title for the lectures, "Philosophy for the People," reflected his restored hope for a practical path. The next year Emerson was appointed an overseer of Harvard College, a seat that in relatively short order provided him the opportunity of bringing together the various aspects of that project most dear to his heart. The president of the College, Charles Eliot, envisioned a course of "University Lectures" as part of his attempt to establish a graduate program in the liberal arts. He invited Emerson to be one of the seven lecturers on philosophy, and the elder statesman of American letters was allowed to choose his topic. Thus did "The Natural History of the Intellect" become a course of sixteen lectures in the spring of 1870. The task of assembling several decades of material from journals, notebooks, and lectures,—of arranging, outlining, writing and editing,—proved a monumental task, perhaps the most significant and concentrated project he had yet attempted. Having struggled his way through the spring lectures, Emerson undertook the task of a comprehensive revision of the course that fall, appreciative that the scale and pace of the lectures had left him at a disadvantage to do his best work. After three lectures a week for six weeks, including one where he left the hall in mid-thought and another where he simply failed to show, he apologetically assured one of the students that next year would be better. In 1871 he gave his final presentation of his best thoughts on the topic that he had pursued for thirty-three years. The present volume is the first time the 1871 cycle of seventeen lectures has been published. It represents the fullest expression of Emerson's attempt to fulfill the chief task of his life.

These lectures must not be viewed as the actual fulfillment of the task that Emerson had set for himself. Such a deed would have required Emerson to turn his lectures into essays, as he had done so many times earlier in his career,—to fill the page with the character of the writer, as he was wont to express it. The goal of the lecture, from Emerson's viewpoint, was somewhat different from that of the essay. Had he had the opportunity to take that final step with the *Natural History*, the final version would have been markedly different from what is contained in this volume. He described the purpose of a lecture as the experience, for both speaker and audience, of "l'abandon," a moment he always awaited when lecturing, for "in perfect eloquence, the hearer would lose the sense of dualism of hearing from another; would cease to distinguish between orator and himself; would have the sense only of high activity and progress." With this Emersonian distinction between essay and lecture in mind, the reader of the 1871 cycle,— using imagination as that power of the mind able to transport him or her into the audience at Harvard on those spring days of 1871,— may be able to sense how the written words were, for Emerson, building blocks of Discourse that enabled him to construct a spiritual temple for the Intellect. Each lecture allowed the hearer to experience the descent of the Idea, the living thought, into the home and hall that Emerson had prepared for it.

The concept of the Intellect to which Emerson was devoted

is paradoxical in that it is better grasped as an experience than as an idea. The Intellect played a central role in the philosophy of Neo-Platonism, whose primary exponents were Philo, Plotinus, and Proclus,—names which Emerson included in his 1841 essay on "Intellect." While these thinkers are generally looked down on by more traditional philosophers, Emerson extolled their brilliance and connected their efforts to the works of the pre-Socratic philosophers, such as Heraclitus, and their predecessors in Egypt, such as Hermes Trismegistus. In 1870 he went so far as to devote one of the concluding lectures of the cycle, entitled "Platonists," to a study of the importance of that school. Emerson had planned to deliver the lecture in 1871 as well, but ultimately had to cut it from the final cycle because of time constraints. Cabot, himself a philosopher and one of the six other lecturers who participated in the University Courses of 1870-71, tended to share the prevailing attitude toward the Neo-Platonists, the view that the epithet given to Heraclitus—the Obscure—was appropriate.

Undoubtedly it was Emerson's insistence on basing his "philosophical" project—what he sometimes referred to as the "New Metaphysics"—on the ideals of the Platonists, as well as his apparent inability to define the concept of the Intellect in a philosophically satisfactory way, that led Cabot to conclude that, for thirty-three years of trying, Emerson had only succeeded in making an initial start towards a useful framework of thought. When Cabot prepared the 1883 edition of Emerson's *Complete Works*, the 1871 lectures had no place in it. He eventually changed his mind about withholding Emerson's chief task from the public; in 1893 he published a new, twelfth volume of the *Works* that bore the title "The Natural History of the Intellect." Yet these were not the Harvard lectures. To avoid embarrassment, as he supposed, to the family, Cabot had lent Emerson a hand. What he produced was a strange patchwork, a heavily-edited compilation of Emerson's several attempts to give the "Natural History" over the years that drew only a small fraction of its content from the 1871 lectures. In a certain way he was trying to re-create Emerson's method of transforming lectures into essays by extracting what he considered to be the best pieces and assembling them anew in a logical order. What the surgical Cabot apparently failed to grasp was that the significance of the "Natural History" to Emerson was in the organic growth of the project over thirty-three years to new plateaus and vistas of thought. The age of the thought in his mind—where he arrived at life's end, rather than where he had been—expressed all the value to be had. In the spring of 1871, Emerson had presented his philosophy for the people—his matured understanding of a path of self-development for the common citizen.

In his attempts to lay out such a path and explore the Constitution of Man, Emerson considered the enumeration of the powers of the mind to be the most daunting task. Describing these powers accurately and plainly had been a challenge from his earliest efforts at the project. Emerson did not view them as abstractions or mental models, but as tools for knowing the very inwardness of things—true faculties of perception. The activity of the Intellect in the human soul became the central theme of the first half of the 1871 cycle (lectures 1-9). He began in the first lecture ("Introductory") by introducing the Beatitude of Intellect and characterizing this high state of consciousness, often called Intuition, as a living into the spiritual environment, as a standing on the bank of the stream of thought. The following lecture, "The Transcendency of Physics," characterized an even higher state of consciousness, an experience of the correspondences of macrocosm and microcosm, of the laws of nature and those of the mind. The following lectures included descriptions and insights into those more familiar psychic states called "Imagination" (lecture 5) and "Inspiration" (lecture 7), as well as an extended two-part study of the elusive and little-understood power of human "Memory" (lectures 4 and 6). Emerson completed this survey of the powers of the mind by examining the everyday consciousness from the perspective of the Intellect in "Instinct and Perception" (lecture 3), "Common Sense" (lecture 8), and "Wit and Humor" (lecture 9). While his contemporaries may have looked at Emerson's exploration of the powers of the mind askance, modern readers may recognize his terms more readily and find his approach to self-development to be quite timely. Even more significant to present day readers are Emerson's warnings about the dangers of subaltern methods of scrying into the spiritual world, such as mesmerism and other lost arts described in "Demonology" (lecture 11).

Emerson began the second half of the 1871 cycle by looking at the activity of the Intellect in the human soul as an outward

result, as the appearance of the Intellect in nature and human society. "Genius" (lecture 10) took up the human experience of the
divine within; Emerson even used the Greek word, "apotheosis," to
help explain the deification of man possible through the gradual
process of self-development. Together with "Transcendency of
Poetry" and "Laws of Mind," lectures 10, 12, and 13 exemplify
Emerson's tripartite understanding of the Intellect as the Doer in
the realm of willing and deliberate action, the Sayer in the poetic
realm of feeling, and the Knower in the ordered realm of pure
thinking. Following these lectures, Emerson offered his insight into
the human race as a whole in "Metres of Mind" (lecture 14) as he
presented the idea of Leonardo da Vinci, that humanity actually
constitutes a fourth kingdom of nature and that each individual is
a species unto him or herself. He explained how the idea of Michael
Faraday,—that the law of magnetism applies not just to metals but
to the whole mineral realm,—could be raised up and grasped as a
law of the mind, as the law of bias whereby "every soul has a bias or
polarity of its own ... everyone is a magnet with a new north." Cast-
ing this insight into his own words, Emerson posed his belief "that
each soul represents a certain fact in nature, a law, sometimes a fact
in natural science or in politics or in morals, a law of beauty, or of
metaphysics, or of mechanic power whose demonstrator or orator
he is and should be, that justice may be done to that particular fact
among men." The Intellect in history, he had observed, makes its
kings, its generals, its presidents—every eye placed in exactly the
right place to testify of a particular ray of light. In a similar a way,

Emerson viewed himself as the orator of the Intellect. His life task was the expression of this one thought that lay ever before his gaze.

The 1871 cycle concluded with a study of the activity of the Intellect in history. Ideas,—not intellections but living thoughts,— were the intermediaries of the Intellect in the realm of history, and the "Conduct of Intellect" (lecture 16) revealed how "an idea over-hangs like the moon, and rules the tide which rises simultaneously in all the souls of a generation." In the history of ideas, those of greatest power and moment enter civilization through the poet, and thus poetry governs every people. Emerson noted that the appearance of such an idea on the shores of the American conti-nent occurred through the Declaration of Independence, and the idea that "all men are created equal" became the lodestone of the Republic. To conclude the course, Emerson delved into the "Rela-tion of Intellect and Morals" (lecture 17) and showed advances in history to be a kind of moral evolution led by men of conscience. The lecture ended with the exemplum of the advocate of the good cause, John Brown of Ossawotomie, and how Truth and Nature helped him to preserve the Idea of the Founders for his own generation.

There are various reasons that *The Natural History of the Intellect* had to wait 137 years for its publication. The lectures made their way from Cabot to Emerson's son, Edward, who published a new edition of his father's *Complete Works* but did little with the "Natural History" beyond his predecessor's efforts. Eventually the manuscripts were deposited at Harvard's Houghton Library along with the bulk of Emerson's papers and entrusted to the care of the Ralph Waldo Emerson Memorial Association. As volume after volume of journals, letters, and other unpublished work came out over the succeeding decades to illuminate Emerson's life and thought, the only insight into the Natural History project was ten pages about the 1870 cycle and a bare sentence about the 1871 cycle in Cabot's *Memoir*, followed by the curious pseudo-essay published in the 1893 *Complete Works*. For a hundred years, Cabot's was the last word on Emerson's "Cambridge Course." Emerson scholars, by and large, had to accept Cabot's assessment of the work or make the journey to Houghton Library and attempt the manuscripts for themselves. Some went so far, on the information at hand, as to doubt the importance of the project; others chose to ignore it altogether or offer merely passing recognition.

Had they traveled to Cambridge to look at the original lectures, curious readers would have found twenty folders, seemingly in chaotic disarray, written in a sprawling hand that is often barely legible—apparently a hopeless mix of complete and partial lectures left over from both the 1870 and 1871 cycles. To make matters worse, the loose sheets of paper, more often than not, bear multiple conflicting page numbers (for it was Emerson's practice to re-use the same sheet of writing over and over again in different contexts) and have no binding to indicate a comfortable order. The hopeless sense of disorder is made complete with the presence in the folders not only of the text of the lectures, but of Emerson's notes and outlines as well, which he had left in place apparently in hopes that they would be useful in later forming a series of essays. Only a few of the lectures are clearly written out on numbered pages or unencumbered by sheets of notes. Few scholars or biographers attempted the folders. The current editors found the majority of the lectures still not microfilmed, the only way to study the lectures outside of Houghton's reading room. Those scholars that did view the folders generally came away disheartened or simply mystified. The last ten years has seen renewed critical interest in the Natural History project, even witnessing the publication of the 1848 and 1858 cycles, though the 1866 and 1870-71 lectures have remained hidden from the public.[†] There is not space here to delve into the textual problems presented by the manuscript. The interested reader may find a review of the literature, the story of our own engagement with the lectures, our case for presuming that the lectures are intact, and complete documentation of our editorial process and decisions, in addition to redacted material, in the critical edition of the lectures, *Natural History of the Intellect: Emerson's Cambridge Course of 1871*, forthcoming from the Wrightwood Press.

The current volume represents seven years of research, editing, and revision upon revision. The nature of the manuscript is such that just when an editor believes he has come to an under-

---

† Of note are the interest that Robert Richardson takes of the lectures in his biography, *Emerson: the Mind on Fire*; Ronald Bosco's transcript of student notes of the 1870 lectures published in the Harvard Library Bulletin, v.8, no. 2; and Bosco and Meyerson's edition of *The Later Lectures of Ralph Waldo Emerson*.

standing of Emerson's intention, a word or page will reveal itself to be entirely different from what it first seemed and illuminate the passages around it with new context and meaning. At the forefront of our efforts has been an aim for integrity and fidelity to Emerson's original intent for the lectures. The editorial standards maintained by generations of Emerson scholars have been our constant guide, though we have parted with conventional wisdom on the recoverability of the cycle as Emerson delivered it in the spring of 1871. Every interpretation or emendation has been submitted to a second pair of eyes, often for repeated evaluation, and every disputed paragraph, sentence, clause, and comma has been deferred to the original manuscript for resolution.

Outside of the editing room, many hands have helped this project on its way. We are particularly grateful to Stuart Weeks and the Center for American Studies for the generous grant that enabled us to complete the first phase of transcription and editing. Special thanks are due to Leslie Morris, Curator of Manuscripts and Rare Books at Houghton Library, for her steadfast interest and assistance over the years, and to the board of the Ralph Waldo Emerson Memorial Association, who have made this publication possible. Ronald Bosco introduced us to the notes of two students who attended the 1870 series, which led to numerous indispensable insights that helped unravel the Gordian knot of the manuscripts and illuminate the evolution of the 1870 lectures into those of 1871. Robert Richardson provided counseling and advice as we explored various avenues for bringing the lectures forward.

We are greatly indebted to Kay and Graham Evans, who graciously allowed their dining room to become something of a fortified camp on more than one occasion. Jennifer Greene has been a mainstay of support and enthusiasm, our constant advisor and champion of the work. Our deepest thanks are reserved for Alice and Dasa, who have weathered cross-country trips, long hours, and occasional apparent madness, and returned bottomless support and understanding year in and year out, to the perpetual enrichment of our efforts.

# Cambridge Course

*Harvard University*
*1871*

# INTRODUCTORY

*February 14, 1871*

◦~

*"It was long ago in a full senate of all intellects determined how cocoons had best be suspended; kindred mind with mine that admires and approves decided it so. The mind of the universe, which we share, has been intended on each particular object."*

—H.D. Thoreau

THE BEATITUDE OF INTELLECT,—TIS TOO GREAT FOR FEEBLE souls. The wineglass shakes, and the wine is spilled. What then? The joy which will not let me sit in my chair, nor lie in my bed, which brings me upright to my feet, and I cannot have composure and concentration enough to set down in English words the thought which thrills me,—is not that joy a measure of the rank of the thought? What if I never write or read again? For a moment, the eyes of my eyes were opened, the affirmative experience remains, and consoles through all events.

There is no wise man; men are vascular only; constructive men only; cups or pipes; through which the stream rolls today, to roll tomorrow through others, and leave these dry. As high as thy knowledge goes, thou canst not overpraise the great; yet are there as much greater beyond. Thy feet are on the lowest round of the ladder and before the Deity thy gods are puppets. But here shall weakness treat of force. I dare not deal with this element in its pure essence. It is too rare for the wings of words, and one must not speak of the moment except in the moment. Yet I see that Intellect is a science of degrees, and that, as man is conscious of the law of vegetable and animal nature, so he is aware of an Intellect which overhangs his consciousness like a sky, of degree above degree, and heaven within heaven. In its last aspect, it is the supreme fact we know, is the commander of matter, and is the life and order by which matter exists. It was described by the ancient as the *To κινητικον*,[†] that which is moved by itself. There is nothing else which moves itself except soul.

It is a steep stair down from this essence of Intellect Pure, to thought or intellections. As the sun is conceived to have made our system by hurling from itself the outer rings of diffuse ether which slowly condensed into earths and moons,—by a higher force of the same law, the mind detaches minds, and a mind detaches thoughts or intellections. These again mimic in their sphericity, the first mind, and share its power.

And what are thoughts? They are perceptions of single relations of the laws of nature. It is the necessity of the human mind to see in succession the facts or laws of nature, as the eye looks at one or another object. It is higher to prefer thoughts to politics, manual

---

† Prime Mover

skill, money; higher yet to prefer ideas to thoughts. Who has ever found its boundaries?

I knew a student who sat long at the door; gladly he would dedicate himself to such a god, be a fakeer of the Intellect, fast and pray, spend and be spent, pay the dread taxes which Nemesis exacts of the class, wear its colors, pallor, sterility, celibacy, poverty, insignificance, were these the livery of its troop, honest infirmities, honorable scars, so that he be rewarded by conquest of principles; or, by being purified and admitted into the immortalities, mount and ride on the backs of these thoughts,—steeds which course forever the ethereal plains. Time was nothing; centuries and cycles were well wasted in these surveys. It seemed as if the sentences he wrote, a few sentences,—after summers of contemplation,—shone again with all the suns which had risen and set to contribute to his knowing. Few, few were the lords he could reckon, Perception, Memory, Imagination, and the sky of Reason over all. He did not know more for living long.

Higher than all feats of talent is the intellect itself: intellections are external to intellect, a heaven within man, a realm of undiscovered sciences, of slumbering potences, a heaven of which the feats of talent are no measure: it arches like a sky over all that it has done, all that has been done. All that is urged by the Saint for the superiority of faith over works, is as truly urged for the highest state of intellectual perception, over any intellectual performance. In excited conversations, we have glimpses of the universe, perceptions of immense power native to the first, far-darting lights and shadows of a mountain landscape, such as we cannot often attain unto in our solitary studies. In Faneuil Hall, or in the Senate house, we look for powerful statement and broad political views. But suddenly in your parlor you shall find your companion sitting by your side start up a more potent man than Demosthenes, and on the instant, make London and Washington politics appear old carrion and dust heaps, because his suggestions require new ways of living, new books, new men, new arts and sciences.

For my thoughts, I seem to stand on the bank of a river, and watch the endless flow of the stream floating objects of all shapes, colors and natures; nor can I much detain them as they pass, except by running beside them a little way along the bank. But whence they come, or whither they go, is not told me. Only I have a suspicion that, as geologists say that every river makes its own valley, so does this mystic stream. It makes its valley, makes its banks, and makes, perhaps, the observer too. And James Very, when I charged him with being sensitive and tenacious of certain expressions in his poems, replied, "I value them, not because they are mine, but because they are not." As soon as the intellect awakes all things are changed; all things, the most familiar, make a musical impression. Sometimes tis comedy without laughter. Every creature in the human world, fashionist, farmer, millionaire, pauper, magistrate, all are toy-people in a toy-house.

Dionysius described the orders of celestial angels, so the degrees of Intellect are an organic fact, and it is these which give birth to mythology. You have been pleased with stories of gods, in

Homer, Ovid, and the Edda. I invite you to the beholding and knowing of real gods, who forever work and rule: Memory; and Vision; the Power of Imagination; the Poet Apollo, the Zodiacal Chain of Cause and Effect; Illusion the veil, and Transition the Energy; Wisdom with his solar eye, whose look is classification, and distributes natures. And high over all its several perceptions and powers, the Intellect Pure, which we cannot discriminate from the Cause of Causes.

We have had our Jonathan Edwards, but young America is not fond of metaphysics. It is to the youth a manilla full of pepper, and he wants only a teaspoonful in a year. So he admires the Dutch who burnt half the harvest, and enhanced the remainder beyond the value of the whole. Tis thus with ontology. Dreary are the names and numbers of volumes of Kant, Schelling, Hegel and the Hegelians to him who only wants to know at the shortest the few steps, the two steps, or the one actual step by the most advanced mind. We know what step Berkeley took, and we recognize the same in the Hindoo books. Hegel took a second step and said that there are two elements, something and nothing, and that the two are indispensable at every subsequent step as much as at the first. Well, we have familiarized that dogma and at least conceded a kind of necessity in it, even if poor human nature still feels the paradox.

Now is there any third step which Germany has made of like importance and renown? It certainly needs no encyclopedia of volumes to tell. We want not the metaphysics, but the result,—or shall I say, only the literature of them; the man who can humanize this fine science, and give us the results. The adepts only value, and rightly, the pure geometry, the aerial or ideal bridge ascending from earth to heaven, with arches and abutments of pure reason. We are fully contented if you tell us where are the true termini.

I find some recoil upstream a little uncanny. I think tis better to follow its waters on their way into life,—to see the powers in governing kingdoms, organizing society, in arts, in science, in poetry, in life, for in all these we go to the end of use. So Swedenborg upheaved the law out of piety. Goethe had this feeling. But I share the wonder and awe of the fact when I see the outpouring,—when I see the thought poured into man, unlocking nature; every thought symboled by nature; every fact in nature a type of somewhat in him.

# TRANSCENDENCY OF PHYSICS

*February 17, 1871*

❦

*An apothegm has come down to us as one of the few re-
maining fragments of the very earliest philosophy, "that
there is nothing on earth which is not in the heavens in a
heavenly form, and nothing in the heavens which is not on
the earth in an earthly form."*

"THERE IS A CERTAIN COMMON BOND THAT UNITES ALL THE
sciences together," said Cicero, or as a Frenchman would say, all the
sciences are *solidaires*. The same genius breathes through them all,
and they are successive planes and forms for the appearance of the
same power. The highest value of natural history, of the new results
of geology, of the discovery of parallax, and the resolution of neb-
ulae is its translation into an universal cipher applicable to the
Intellect. "All the languages should be studied abreast," said Krait-
sir; and all the sciences should be, and all illuminate each other.
"Teach me the laws of music," said Fourier, "and I can tell you any
secret in any part of the universe, in anatomy, for instance, or in
astronomy." Kepler thought as much. Agassiz told me that when
he was at a loss in his study of embryos, he would go and talk with
astronomers about the nebular theory, what occurred in such and

such conditions of the forming planet, and presently he got the analogic hint he wanted. Homology is the great gain of modern science.

There is a similarity of intellect to the history of material atoms. From whatever side we look at nature we seem to be exploring the figure of a disguised man. The world may be reeled off from any one of its laws, like a ball of yarn. The chemist can explain by his analogies the processes of intellect; the zoologist from his; geometer, mechanician respectively from theirs. Thus the idea of vegetation is irresistible in considering mental activity. Man, a higher plant, repeats in his mental functions germination, growth, state of melioration, crossings, blight, parasites, and all the accidents of the plant. Thus a good work does itself,—the new study, the good book, advances, whether the writer is awake or asleep. Our mental processes go forward when they seem suspended. Scholars say that, if they return to the study of a new language after some intermission, the intelligence of it is more and not less. A subject of thought to which we return from month to month, from year to year, has always some new ripeness of which we can give no account. Hence we say, the book grew in the author's mind. There is always a new thought awaiting us in the morning, as the plant during the night has put out a new leaf.

Our mental words are derived from the animal body as, grasp, carry, leap, swallow, digest, run, sleep, wake, hear. And in the impenetrable mystery which hides (and hides through absolute transparency) the mental nature, I await the insight which our advancing knowledge of material laws shall furnish. Thus the laws of fluids, and the atmosphere, of light, heat, electricity, and galvanism, the laws of undulation and polarity, are symbolical statements of the laws of memory and of thinking. So the relation between intellect and morals is like that between light and heat. Modern philosophers have established the identity of light and heat. The same force, combined with body, is heat; thrown off from body, is light.

Napoleon sees one character running through all modes of war. "Whatever they may tell you, believe that one fights with cannon as with fists." I find it easy to translate all his technics into all of mine; and Carnot's and Maupertuis' laws of dynamics; and the laws of architecture; and the rest. Every breath of air is a carrier of the universal mind. For all difference is quantitative: the quality is one. Carnot added a new theorem to dynamics which was in sum, that sudden alterations of speed are to be avoided in machinery because all the power that in the moment of stoppage is taken from the legitimate action of the machine goes to tear the machine asunder. When he was counseled to break up the French Directory he replied, "No, for sudden losses of speed are damaging." He too was a poet, and universalized his propositions. Maupertuis taught that the power employed in nature to produce a change in the movement of bodies is always a minimum. Voltaire says he was a fop, and it is true that he got himself painted with the globe, oblate spheroid, patted in his hand. And I have heard it announced as a thesis in Zoology that, in nature, there is a minimum of pain; that the bird of prey seizes its victim in the manner that kills with the least suffering, and the fact which Dr. Livingston reports that when struck by the paw of a lion, he became fearless, as if fascinated.

All thought analogizes. Mental faculties are the transcendency of the physical. All above as below is organized, and after one law, so that whoso enunciates a law of nature—in the same words enunciates a law of the mind.

The laws of material nature, (namely, chemistry, polarity, undulation, gravity, centrifugence, periodicity) run up into the invisible world of the mind. And hereby we acquire a key to those sublimities which skulk and hide in the caverns of human consciousness, namely by the solar microscope of *Analogy*. Tis the key that opens the universe. Nature shows everything once, shows everything in coarse or colossal lines somewhere; and here, by extending into our reveries and dreams the same law by which tides ebb and flow, moons wax and wane, trees grow, and stones fall. Those laws of chemistry, astronomy, botany are repeated on a higher plane in the mind. Thus the first quality we know in matter is centrality, which we commonly call gravity, and which holds the Universe, pure and indestructible in motes, as in masses, and from each atom rays out illimitable influence. To this central essence answers truth in the intellectual world,—Truth, whose centre is everywhere, and its circumference nowhere; whose existence we cannot disimagine; Truth, the soundness and health of things, against which no blow can be struck, but it recoils on the striker; no fraud can prosper. Liars also are true. Let a man begin where he will, and work in whatever direction, he is sure to be found instantly afterwards arriving at a right result. Truth, which we cannot wound, on whose side we always heartily are.

And, as gravity is a primal attribute of matter, so a primal measure of a mind is its centrality, its veracity, its entire yielding to a grander gravity, namely, to the reality and essence of things, which we call truth. Like the momentum of falling bodies, the power of the mind, and its pace, increases as it approaches the end of its task. The momentum which increases by exact law in falling bodies increases by the like ratio in mental action. Every scholar knows, that he applies himself coldly and slowly at first, but, with the progress of the work, the mind becomes heated, and sees far and wide as it approaches the end of the task, so that it is the common remark of the student, "Could I only have begun with the same fire I had on the last day I should have done something!" Then to do something well, we must have done it often.

When we have gravity or centrality in nature, then we have Polarity. As one is the principle of rest and permanence, so is this the principle of difference, of generation, of change. In the imponderable fluids, it shows itself in circulation, in undulation, in fits of easy transmission and reflection. In chemistry, it appears in the affinities; in organized matter, in sex. This is not less the essential property of mental life, the flowing, the genesis, the melioration, the advance everlasting. All things flow, said the ancient; $\Pi \alpha \nu \tau \alpha$ $\rho \varepsilon \iota$. The universe is only in transit, or we behold it shooting the gulf from past to future. And this the mind shares. Transition is the attitude of power, and the essential act of life. The whole history of the mind is passage, pulsation, dark and light, preparation and arrival, and again, preparation and arrival. We are passing into new earths and new heavens,—into new earths, by chemistry; into new heavens, in fact, by the movement of our solar system, and in thought, by our better knowledge.

See how the organism of the mind corresponds to that of the body. There is the same hunger for food,—we call it curiosity. There is the same swiftness of seizing it,—we call it perception; the same assimilation of food to the eater,—we call it culture. For, simple recipiency is the virtue of space, not of a man. But, as it is a law that "two great sexes animate the world," we note that a powerful mind impresses itself on a whole nation of minds and is the parent of an innumerable spiritual progeny. Count the census of the Platonists; of the Aristotelian minds; of the followers of St. Paul; of Luther; of Descartes; of Voltaire; of Swedenborg; of Goethe, and it is a genetic or organic difference and may surely be predicted before they are acquainted with these masters. Again, Nature loves to cross her stocks; and does the variety and blending of talents less appear in new minds that have been bred under varied and antagonistic influence,—under Napoleon, and under Goethe? Thirty years ago, Germany divided itself complexionally into disciples of Goethe and Schiller. Composite minds, like Burke, which blend two tendencies or strains of thought, give a rich result; and usually every mind of remarkable efficiency owes it to new combination of traits.

The phenomenon of sex reappears in male and female minds,

which by no means follow the sex of the body. One mind is creative or a male mind; the other is apprehensive or a female mind: and the equality of the sexes establishes itself here again, for we have often occasion to remark the equality of a profound apprehension to the greatest poet. The creative seems mere knack. The gestation or bringing forth of the mind is seen in the act of detachment. Life is incessant parturition. There are viviparous and oviparous minds, minds that produce their thoughts complete men, like armed soldiers, ready and swift to resist and conquer all the armies of error; and others that deposit their dangerous unripe thoughts here and there to lie yet for a time and be brooded in other minds, and the shell shall not be broken until the next age that they may begin, as new individuals, their career. Some minds suffocate from too much store, too little vent. Kvasir, in the Norse legend, was a man so wise that none asked him anything which he knew not how to answer; but the dwarves said, that he had choked in his wisdom, there being none wise enough to ask him enough about learning. Health consists in the balance between knowing and expression,—in keeping the channels open. Some minds choke from too much; some pine from too little communication. Some discharge their thought in volleys; and I am sure that I could point to others by name who would be invaluable, if you could attach to them a self-acting siphon that would tap and draw them off, as now they carry about with them a perilous wisdom, which they have no talent to impart.

All natural functions are attended by their own pleasure,— so are metaphysical. Perception gives pleasure; classification gives a keen pleasure. Memory does; Imagination intoxicates. See how nature has secured the communication of knowledge. Tis certain, that money does not more burn in a boy's pocket, than a piece of news burns in our memory, until we can tell it. And in higher activity of the mind, every new perception is attended with a thrill of pleasure, and the imparting of it to others is also attended with pleasure. Thought is the child of the Intellect, and the child is conceived with joy, and born with joy.

In chemistry, the fermentations go on, the saccharine and vinous, the acetous, and the solid lump irresistibly mounts into gas, and who knows?—into the imponderables. Every material possession must pass into the intellect to become of real value. Until we have intellectual property in a thing, we can have no right property in it. So works the poor little blockhead manikin. He must arrange and classify his shop or farm, the best he can. At last, he must be able to tell you it, or write it, or to himself translate it all clumsily enough into the new sky-language he calls thought. Say not tis bungling: he can't help it. The irresistible meliorations bear him forward. The fermentations go on, saccharine and vinous now, acetous by and by, upward to gas, and the imponderables, at last.

There are those who disputing will make you dispute, and the nervous and hysterical and animalized will produce a like series of symptoms in you, though no other persons ever evoke the like phenomena in you, and though you are conscious that they do not properly belong to you, but are a sort of extension of the diseases of this particular party into you. There are certain ridiculous and incredible sympathies known to physicians. And is it not said to be a law of bodies, which Liebig affirmed,—the contagious influence of chemical action,—that a body in the act of combination or decomposition enables another body, with which it is in contact, to enter into the same state? A substance which would not itself yield to a particular chemical attraction, will do so, if placed in contact with some other body which is in the act of yielding to the same force. Intellectual activity is contagious, like the superinductions of chemistry. Napoleon napoleonizes you, and Plato platonizes you, and a blockhead makes a blockhead of you for the time. It is sufficient almost to set any susceptible soul in the mood of writing verses,—merely to read any original stirring poetry. And it is only necessary to look at the current literature to see how one masterpiece brings into vogue a whole catalogue of books in the same style. What an impulse Linnaeus, Hunter, Oken, Cuvier, Goethe, Robert Brown, Hutton, Von Buch, have given to science! The spectacle of vigor of any kind recruits us. In unfit company, the finest powers are benumbed, and no aids avail to resist the palsy of misassociation.

It is observed that, as there are times of famine, of pest and cholera in races, so there are epochs of decline of genius and destitution of thought. It has been noticed that these times precede as a cause such national calamities. It is a hibernation or sleep of the mind. But the same periodicity which governs the ebb and flow of seas and the astronomic motion reaches also into the laws of thought. Each produces the other. The mind now retires inward, to a sort of hibernation, sheds her plumes, hoards by coarse activity, to be freed again for new power in science and art; and this alternation of animal and of intellectual eras follows on the other. The spiritual crises are states of as certain recurrence in some form to every mind, as are dentition and puberty.

The *first day* of consciousness is when the young child first *finds himself*, as we say; the *second day* of youth, when the mind begins to render account to itself, when it assumes its own vows, when its religious convictions befall; the day of love, when it joins itself to its kind; and the day of reason, when it sees all its partial and fiery experiences as elements of its genius and destiny.

This primary alternation, this come and go, ebb and flow, sleep and waking, the "fits of easy transmission and reflection," the pendulum, the pulse, the undulation, which shows itself as a fundamental secret of nature, exists in intellect.

> The circulation of the waters. The rain falls, the brook runs into the river, the river into the sea; the sea exhales all day its steam into the air. The universal vegetation sucks the stream, and gives it again to the atmosphere. It gathers into clouds, and drifts to the mountains, and falls in rain, to renew its round.

> The circulation of the air. Gas locked up in blocks of basalt, in globe-crusts of granite, in beds of coal that floor counties and states, then heaved in new ages, and unlocked by chemic affinities,—and the joyful vesicle

with all its eternal properties safe and sound,—there is no tear or wear to it,—through all its changes indestructible;—millions of years old, but as good as new,—sails away to enter into new combining,—to make part of the plant; then part of the animal that feeds on it; then part of man that feeds on the animal; then, by and by, buried once more in stone, inundated by new seas; for more millions of years; to wait for new fires to lift it again to repeat the like circulation.

The circulation of the blood in the little world of man,—food into chyme, chyme into chyle, chyle into blood, hurled from the heart in endless spasm to rush through the system, carrying nutriment to every organ and every extremity.

Not less large, not less exact, are the mysterious circulations in the realm of mind. The perceptions of a soul,— its wondrous progeny,—are born by the conversation, the marriage of souls, so nourished, so enlarged. They are detached from their parent; they pass into other minds; ripened and unfolded by many; they hasten to incarnate themselves in action, to take body, only to carry forward the will which sent them out. They take to themselves wood, and stone, and iron, ships, and cities, armies, and nations of men, ages of duration, the pomps of religion, the armaments of war, the codes and heraldry of states, agriculture, trade, colonies,—these are the ponderous instrumentalities into which these nimble thoughts pass, and which they animate and alter, and presently antagonized by other thoughts which they first aroused, or by thoughts which are sons and daughters of these, the thought buries itself only in the new thought of larger scope which sprang from it, only in its own new creations and forwarder triumphs; whilst the old instrumentalities and incarnations are decomposed and recomposed into new.

# Instinct and Perception

*February 21, 1871*

❧

*Perception exists only while used. "The essence of mind,"
said Descartes, "consists in thinking, as that of matter in
extension."*

A LITTLE FINER ORDER, A LARGER ANGLE OF VISION, COMMANDS centuries of facts and millions of thoughtless people. We shall not long go on reckoning prosperity by the census, but by the competent heads. It is a few heads which carve out this vast business the world so bustles in, with craftsmen, clerks and books. A few men invented the works which all do. There's no prosperity, trade, art, city, or great wealth of any kind, but if you trace it home you will find it rooted in the energy of some individual. Genius is a natural method, or real principle of order. Angleo, Schelling, Napoleon, each is a head coming among confusions, and distributing things hitherto in chaos, after right relations, or in an order which is beauty.

Pure power is best and easiest to carry. Give me Archimedes, Agis, Belisarius, Condé, Nelson, or Bonaparte, and you may have the commissaries and quartermasters. Whilst corn grows, whilst men, wheat, and iron are to be found,—with these men I shall be pretty sure to have them. Newton will not long be a stranger anywhere in the Copernican system. Every peasant turns butter, every acre of ground measures out corn, when the hero arrives.

Tis certain that a man's whole possibility is contained in that habitual first look which he casts on all objects. Here alone is the field of metaphysical discovery and of every religion or civil order that has been or shall be. All that we know is flakes and grains from this mountain.

A day comes when each man detects that there is somewhat in him that knows more than he does. Then he puts the question: Who's who? Which of these two is really me? The one that knows more or the one that knows less? The little fellow, or the big fellow?—Somewhat within him that knows more than he does. A certain dumb life in life, a simple wisdom behind all acquired wisdom; somewhat not educated or educable, not altered or alterable, a mother wit which does not learn by experience, or by books, but knew it all already; makes no progress; does not know more for living long, but was wise in youth as in age. More or less clouded, it yet resides the same in all, saying *Aye* or *No* to every proposition. Yet its grand *Aye* and its grand *No* are more musical than all eloquence. Nobody has found the limits of its knowledge. What object soever is brought before it is already well known to it. The husks that wrap the object shrivel and disappear before its eye; it judges not by quantity, or by form, but by quality. Its justice is perfect; its look is catholic and universal; its light ubiquitous like that of the sun. It does not put forth organs, but rests in presence. Yet, trusted and obeyed in happy natures, it becomes active and salient, and makes new means for its great ends.

This never pretends. Nothing seems less, nothing is more. Ask what the Instinct declares and we have little to say: He is no newsmonger, no disputant, no talker. Tis a taper, a spark in the great night, yet a spark at which all the illumination of human arts and sciences was kindled. This is that glimmer of inextinguishable light by which men are guided. Though it does not show objects, yet shows the way. This is that sense by which men feel when they are wronged, though they do not see how. This is that source of thought and feeling which acts on masses of men,—on all men at certain times,—with resistless power. Ever at intervals leaps a word or fact to light, which is no man's invention, but the common instinct, making the revolutions which never go back. Thus the law of Truth, *Thou shalt not lie*. Thus in the last century, the phrase, "all men are born free and equal," though resisted and denied by all laws and politics, is the keyword to our modern civilization, and in long time is established by all the resistance made to it.

None of the metaphysicians has prospered in describing this power, which constitutes sanity and is the corrector of private excesses and mistakes, public in all its regards, and of a balance which is never lost, not even in the insane. It works by tendency, by surprise, by long bias; its source is deep as the world. This is Instinct, and Inspiration is only the Power excited, breaking its silence; the spark bursting into flame. It belongs to all. It is in the secret of the world. It is in strictest alliance with moral nature: it proceeds from that. It is that which opens to each soul accordingly as it is obeyed, and hereby all contradictions are reconciled. Pan was only seen under disguises, and was not represented by any outward image: a terror sometimes,—at others, a placid omnipotence. Such homage did the Greek, delighting in accurate form, not fond of the extravagant and unbounded, pay to the inscrutable force we call Instinct,—or Nature when it first becomes intelligent.

A man searches his mind for thoughts and finds only the old commonplaces, but, at some moment, on the old topic of the day's astronomy or of politics, he makes a distinction he had not made, he discerns a little inlet not seen before, say Copernicus, or Adam Smith; where was a wall, is now a door. He goes in and out, and variously states in prose or poetry the new experience. He points it out to one or another who each of course deny the alleged discovery. But the repeated experiments and affirmations make it visible soon to others. The point of interest is here—that these gates, once opened, never swing back. The observers may come at their leisure, and do at last satisfy themselves of the fact. The man who opposed you in conversation to extremity, will, afterwards, in his public discourse, temper his own statement so freely with your thought that you find him already half-converted without knowing it. The thought, the doctrine, the right hitherto not affirmed, is published in set propositions, in conversation of scholars, and at last, in the very choruses of songs. The young hear it, and, as they have never fought it, never known otherwise, they accept it, vote for it at the polls, embody it in the laws. And this perception, thus satisfied, re-acts on the senses to clarify them, so that it becomes indisputable at last. Thus it is no matter what the opposition may be of presidents or kings or majorities, but what the truth is, seen by one mind.

The wild pictorial words of the Orientals often come nearer to our experience of the mental phenomena than the painful exact-ness of the German metaphysicians. "A sacred fire without form, shining with a leaping splendor through the profundities of the whole world." This experience no doubt led Plato to say, "Poetry comes nearer to vital truth than history." And Novalis, a profound thinker, said, "The division of philosopher and poet is only appar-ent, not real, and to the disadvantage of both. It is a sign of disease and of a sickly constitution." And let me add for this reason,—that the poet is in the natural attitude, he is believing; the philosopher, after some struggle, having only reasons for believing. It appears at once in the babe: "Like the approach of the iron to the loadstone, is the approach of the new-born child to the breast." Believe the faintest presentiment against the testimony of all history.

Thucydides says, "The Greeks were quick to devise fresh plans (Οξεις εκινοπγαι) and to *anticipate*. Before the orator had finished the first clause of a sentence, they could tell the end." Cer-tain persons utter oracles as Shakespeare, Franklin, Bettine, Margaret Fuller, as real now as of old. We hear, awe-struck, that the Greeks recognized an omen, a *fatum*, now and then in chance words spoken, and we cast about and wonder what these oracles were. And we hear from a companion some remark which explains our own character, or foible, or forte, or circumstance, and it does not occur to us that this is the very chance those ancients considered. This is the omen or *fatum*. But these oracles were in each instance simply perceptions of the Intellect, and whenever the Intellect acts, there is an oracle,—the keen insight into some habit of mind and character betrayed in our act or word, which must have its proper sequel in our fortunes.

## 4

# MEMORY

*February 24, 1871*

〜

I THINK THE MEMORY TOO PRECIOUS A POWER THAN THAT WE can spare any the humblest means that promise to increase or improve it where there is any defect in our constitution that impairs it. Indeed we all of us doubtless have found advantage in some one or other expedient to make the attention more brisk or the tenacity of facts easier. Even trivial expedients are often great helps.

The memory is as the affection. Sampson Reed says, "The true way to store the memory is to develop the affections." A *souvenir* is a token of love. *Remember me* means "Do not cease to love me." We remember those things which we love, and those things which we hate. The memory of all men is robust on the subject of a debt due to them, or of an insult inflicted on them. "They can remember," as Johnson said, "who kicked them last." Every artist is alive on the subject of his art. The Persians finely say, "A real singer will never forget the song which he has once learned."

Memory was called by the schoolmen *vespertina cognitio,*

evening knowledge, in distinction from the command of the future which we have by the knowledge of causes, and which they called *matutina cognitio*, or morning knowledge. Tis because of the believed incompatibility of an affirmative and advancing attitude of mind with tenacious acts of recollection that people are often reproached with living in their memory. But the old rule still stands, that the best security for the memory is really to understand the subject of thought.

The memory is called treacherous. It is a sieve. It is loaded with words and superstitions. It dies in old age. It makes the man of routine. It is jealous of novelties. We say of the sluggish and the obstructionist, he lives in his memory. In the minds of the multitude tis only a calendar. On such a day I paid my note; on the next, took in my coal, sent my cows to pasture, cut my hay, went to Chicago, etc. These are not the faults of the power, but the absence of the power.

Then we forget what ought to be forgotten. What we call the infirmities of memory are not always such, like those of old men who forget names, but not things. How in the right are children to forget name and date and geographic limits, whilst they remember the thread of the story. And if you say, the memory of all men is robust on the debt due to them, or of an insult offered them, we say that with the moral growth, a great soul forgets these also.

We should so gladly find the law of thought unmechanical, but tis a linked chain,—drop out one link, there is no recovery. When newly awaked from lively dreams,—we are so near them, still agitated by them, still in their sphere;—give us one syllable, one feature, one hint, and we should repossess the whole;—hours of this strange entertainment and conversation would come trooping back to us; but we cannot get our hand on the first link or fibre, and the whole is forever lost. What is curious, I have known an instance of a person of accurate perceptions who had mislaid a memorandum, and could not for many days recall what had become of it; but one night dreamed of it, and of the book in which she had laid it, and in the morning, went straight to the book, and found the lost paper in it.

It sometimes occurs that Memory has a personality of its own, and volunteers or refuses its information at *its* will, not at mine. I ask myself: Is it not an old Aunt who goes in and out of the house and occasionally recites anecdotes of old times and persons which I recognize as having heard before,—and, she being gone again, I search in vain for any trace of the anecdotes?

A man would think twice about learning a new science or reading a new paragraph if he believed that the magnetism was only a constant amount and that he lost a word therefore for every word he gained. But the experience is not quite so bad. In reading a foreign language, every new word added is a lamp lighting up related words and so assisting the memory and the apprehension: and so is it with each fact in a new science. The words are mutually explaining, and every one adds transparency to the whole mass.

Are there two memories, the spontaneous and the voluntary? In my dreams, I recall perfectly the voice and language of people, whom I know well enough, but can by no means so exquisitely mimic when I am awake,—for was I not the artist as well as the spectator,—actor and audience?

We like longevity, we like every sign of riches and extent of nature in an individual; but most of all we like a great memory. Who has not heard of the ancient examples of the memory; of Themistocles, of Lucius Scipio, who knew the name of every man in Rome; of Seneca, who could say two thousand words at one hearing; of Mithridates, who, in his army of many nations, could speak to every soldier in his own tongue. Scaliger reports of himself that he could in his youth repeat above a hundred verbs having once read them. John Rainolds, who died in 1607, Anthony Wood tells us, was a third university. He alone was a well furnished library full of all faculties, of all studies, of all learning. The memory and reading of that man were near a miracle. Magliabecchi, when his guardian took away the book in which he delighted, wrote if off from memory and defied him.

We remember what we understand and we understand best what we like, for this doubles our power of attention and makes it our own. Captain John Brown of Ossawatomie said he had in Ohio three thousand sheep on his farm, and could tell a strange sheep in his flock as soon as he saw its face. One of my neighbors, a grazier, told me that he should know again every cow, ox, or steer, that he ever saw. Abel Lawton knew every horse that went up and down through Concord to the towns in the country: And in higher examples each man's memory is in the line of his action.

Memory is not dead,—it is acutely and creatively alive. This is the companion, this the tutor, the poet, the library with which you travel. It does not lie,—cannot be corrupted,—reports to you not what you wish, but what really befel. You say, "I can never think of some act of neglect, of selfishness, or of passion, without pain." Well, that is as it should be. That is the police of the universe: the angels are set to punish you but only so long as you are capable of such crime. But in the history of character, the day comes when you are incapable of such crime. Then you suffer no more; you look on it as Heaven looks on it, with wonder at the deed, and with applause at the pain it has cost you.

Memory is not a pocket, but a living instructer with a prophetic sense of the values which he accumulates; a guardian angel set there within you to record your life, and, by recording, to animate you to uplift it. It is a scripture written day by day from the birth of the man, and all the records full of meanings which open as he lives on, explaining each other,—explaining the world to him, and expanding their sense as he advances, until it shall become the whole law of nature and life.

There is much in us not suspected, and a new passion, a new science, an enlarged character lights up the walls and reads the forgotten inscriptions. Old histories are written in the mind in invisible ink. The fire of love will bring out the letters. The new step, the new thought, the new affection is the Parijati tree. You know the Eastern Indian legend—"The smell of the Parijati tree perfumed the earth for three furlongs, and an approach to it enabled every one to recollect the events of a prior existence." Alas! Alas! could not some divine Torrey and Gray obtain slips of the Parijati tree for our Botanic Garden!

Have you not found Memory an apotheosis or deification? The poor, short, lone fact dies at the birth; Memory catches it up into her heaven and bathes it in immortal waters. Then, a thousand times over, it lives and acts again, each time transfigured, ennobled. In solitude, in darkness, we tread over again the sunny walks of youth; confined now in populous streets, you behold again the green fields, the shadows of the grey birches; by the solitary river, hear again the joyful voices of early companions, and vibrate anew to the tenderness and dainty music of the poetry your boyhood fed upon. At this hour, the stream is still flowing, though you hear it not; the plants are drinking their accustomed life, and repaying it with their beautiful forms. But you need not wander thither. It flows for you, and they grow for you, in the returning images of former summers.

Memory has a fine art of sifting out the pain, and keeping all the joy. The spring days when the bluebird arrives have usually only few hours of fine temperature; are sour and unlovely; but when, late in autumn, we hear rarely a bluebird's notes, they are sweet by reminding us of the spring. Well, it is so with other tricks of memory. Of the most romantic fact, the memory is more romantic, and this power of sinking the pain of any experience, and of recalling the saddest with tranquility, and even with a wise pleasure, is familiar.

In low or bad company, the man folds himself in his cloak, withdraws himself entirely from all the doleful circumstance, recalls and surrounds himself with the best company, and the fairest hours of his life: "Passing sweet are the domains of tender memory." We live late in life by memory, and in our solstices or periods of stagnation, we live on our memories as the starved camel lives on his humps.

Memory performs the impossible for man by the strength of his divine arms; holds together the past and the present, beholding both, existing in both, abides in the flowing, and gives continuity and dignity to human life. Hereby only a home is possible; hereby only a new fact has value; hereby am I lodged in a hall filled with pictures which every new day enhances, and to which every new step of the soul in her endless march adds a perspective more sublime. Whenever the Muses sing, Pan spurts poppy juice all about, so that no one who hears them can carry any word away. So of the sybils writing on leaves which the wind scatters. Alcott asked me if the thought clothes itself in words? I answer, yes, but they are instantly forgotten. The difference between man and man is that in one the memory with inconceivable swiftness flies after and recollects these leaves,—flies on wing as fast as that mysterious whirlwind, and the envious fate is baffled.

# Imagination

*February 28, 1871*

∾

THE PRIMARY USE OF A FACT IS LOW; THE SECONDARY USE, AS IT
is a figure or illustration of my thought, is the real value. First, the
fact; second, its impression, or what I think of it. Hence nature was
called "a kind of adulterated reason." Seas, mountains, timber, metals, diamonds and fossils interest the eye, but tis only with some
preparatory or predicting charm. Their real value comes out only
when I hear their meaning made plain in the spiritual truth they
cover.

    The Soul of the World is the right phrase: soul and world:
it holds the two yet is one in the duplex energy. It pours itself
through the universe and is finding ever expression in creating and
compelling men to utter in their articulate fashion of speech and
arts its million particulars of the one fact of Being. Each creature
in the countless creatures,—hydrogen, oxygen, carbon, animal
fibre, rock, plant, animal, mite, insect, fish, mammal, or man,—is
one more or less adequate fruit or representation of it; each is the
emphasis of some one quality,—emphasis of one, but not contra-

diction of any other quality. Each says somewhat that must be told and only becomes false when it exaggerates that, and so resists the rest. In the moment when it pipes too loud on its own key, a new creature confutes the folly by irresistible exhibition of a new part of nature,—the offset and balance to the last.

I know not any problem on which I should more willingly see the Academy appoint a learned Committee to search and report than the origin and history of the Chaldaic oracles.

> The Intelligible is the aliment of the Intelligent. Learn the intelligible since it exists beyond the mind. For the Framer of the world is the mind of the mind.

> Principles, which have understood the intelligible works of the Father, disclosed them in sensuous works as bodies, being thus ferrymen betwixt the Father and matter, and producing manifest images of unmanifest things, and inscribing unmanifest things in the manifest frame of the world.

> There is something intelligible which it behoves thee to understand with the flower of the mind; not with vehemence of intellection, not fixedly, but having a pure turning eye; if thou inclinest thy mind, thou shalt apprehend this also.

> Let the immortal depth of thy soul lead thee.

> The soul of man will in a manner clasp God to herself. Having nothing mortal, she is wholly inebriated by

God. For to the persevering mortal the blessed immortals are swift.

In these Chaldaic oracles we find seductive images which we explore and explore. They afford cheap wit to accurate grammarians, the braggart of common sense, the Philistine; but they charm thoughtful men. They appear to be the speech of a grand poet or seer full of noble insights and sincerities, reported to us by an auditor who only half understood what he heard. A few sentences are matchless, and have passed into literature. But we wait still for the interpreter, and not without hope since the hieroglyphics have been read.

Tis a rule in eloquence that the moment the orator loses command of his audience, the audience commands him. So, in poetry, I observe that the true poet rushes to deliver his thought, and the words and images fly to him to express it; whilst colder moods are forced to respect the ways of saying it, and insinuate, or as it were, muffle the fact to suit the poverty or caprice of their expression, so that they only hint the matter, or insinuate or allude to it, being unable to fuse and mould their words and images to fluid obedience. See how Shakespeare grapples at once with the main problem of the tragedy as in Lear and Macbeth and the opening of Merchant of Venice.

Write that I may know you. Style betrays you, as your eyes do. We detect at once by it, whether the writer has a firm grasp on his fact or thought,—exists at the moment for that alone, or, whether he has one eye apologizing,—deprecatory,—turned on his reader. In proportion always to his possession of his thought, is his defiance of his readers. There is no choice of words for him who clearly sees the truth. That provides him with the best word. A new poet dazzles us with his lustres, the sparkle of new rhetoric, with his gay vocabulary, shop-new,—and it takes some time to see him truly. But I wish to say to him, that I like only the important passages.

> Calm and still light on yon great plain,
> That sweeps with all its autumn bowers,
> And crowded farms and lessening towers,
> To mingle with the bounding main.
>
> —*Tennyson*

A verse is not a vehicle to carry a sentence, as a jewel is carried in a box; the verse must be alive and inseparable from its contents, as the body of man carries the soul with it. In reading prose, I am sensible as soon as a sentence drags, but, in poetry, as soon as one word drags. I might even say, that the rhyme is there in the theme, thought, and image themselves. We even measure the inspiration by the music. In Byron, the rhyme does not suggest restraint, but the utmost freedom, as the rules of the dance do not fetter the good dancer, but exhibit more clearly his natural grace. Thus, the lines in Childe Harold beginning "I've taught me other tongues, and in strange eyes," etc.

Nature holds us hard to the material world, insists on our living, feeding and working in it as if there were no other from youth to manhood and slowly lets us understand that this was fact by fact instruction for the intellectual and the moral heavens. We complain and wonder. "There is nothing existing in human thought, even though relating to the most mysterious tenet of faith, but has combined with it a natural and sensuous image." The priest leads the child or the convert into the brook, and sprinkles him with a few drops of water, whilst he prays for him, to signify that he is washed from his sin, and shall lead a clean life. The groom puts a ring on the bride's finger and gives the bride his own name, to signify that henceforward they have agreed to be one indivisible person. Ardent persons do somewhat like this in many ways. In old times, friends exchanged their names, or broke a ring or a coin into halves, each taking one.

Fancy is wilful,—Imagination is a spontaneous act; Fancy is a play as with dolls and puppets which we choose to call men and women,—Imagination is a perception and affirming of a real relation between a thought and some material fact. Shakespeare's Queen Mab is an example of Fancy. King Lear's sayings are of the Imagination:

> I tax not you, ye elements, with unkindness,
> I never gave you kingdoms, called you children,
> You owe me no subscription.
> And yet I call you servile ministers
> That have with two pernicious daughters joined
> Your high engendered battles gainst a head
> So old and white as this.

He sees the cruel crime with which his mind is surcharged, in whatever nature he looks upon. Fancy relates to surfaces in which a great part of life lies. The lover is rightly said to take a fancy to the hair, eyes, complexion, of the maid. The mind is perpetually provoked to see how all things reflect or image its momentary thought. Whenever this resemblance is real, not playful, and is deep, or pointing at the causal identity, it is the act of Imagination; if superficial, and for entertainment, it is Fancy.

To say Goethe was natural when he conjured the dismal Faust is folly,—and more, to insist that poets be natural in the sense that excuses grossness. We want some other nature besides the worst of this old world. The very design of Imagination, this gift celestial, is to domesticate us in another nature. To say it is not nature because it is not city life, or the common farmer's life, is absurd.

The ideal of existence is the company of a Muse who doesn't wish to wander, whose visits are in secret, who divulges things not to be made popular. Soon as the wings grow which bring the gazing eyes, even these favorites flutter too near the earth. No faculty leads to the invisible world so readily as imagination. Tis one of the greatest problems that these lights and torches are so often unhappy and miserable. Milton wrote incognito, and Tasso expiated his fame in prison, Ovid in exile, and Dante in persecution and banishment. Genius certifies its possession of a thought by translating it into a fact or form which perfectly represents it. Imagination transfigures, so that only the cosmical relations of the object are seen. Personal beauty, when best, has this transcendency. Under calm and precise outline, we are surprised by the hint of the immeasureable and divine.

We toil and sweat and affect to insist on severe concentration and logical continuity. But there is and must be a little air chamber, a sort of tiny Bedlam, in even the naturalist's and mathematician's brain, who arrives at great results. They affect, I know, a sticking to facts: they repudiate all imagination and affection as they would disown stealing. But Cuvier, Oken, Geoffroy St.-Hilaire, Richard Owen, Agassiz, must all have this spark of fanaticism, for the generation of mental steam, and there must be that judicious tubing in their brain that is in the boiler of the locomotive, or wherever steam must be swiftly generated. They all deny it, of course. Goethe had this air-chamber so large that, like Pericles, he must have a helmet to conceal the dreaded infirmity, but he never owned it,—even would have persuaded the people that it was the county jail. If you have ever so much faculty of detail, without his explosive gas, it makes the Doctor Dryasdusts, the most tedious and dreaded of mankind. But add this fanaticism, and you have Keplers, Linnaeus, Buffons, and Huxleys.

I find I have not said all which I wished in regard to Imagination, and the important part it plays in the intellectual powers. I shall best attempt it by speaking of that form which it takes from the beginning of the world until now in literature. There never was a time when poetry was not. The children were sung to in the cradle. The religion had its songs and prayers. Cleave to truth, and to God, against the name of God. That makes the sublime history of martyrs in philosophy and in religion. How contagious is all mental vigor. How we are shamed by great biographies of those stalwart souls who never quailed or faltered.

Poetry has now a permissive rank, as the bishops of England in the House of Lords. And society is slow to find that it has led and should lead the civilization and politics and religion of mankind. The poet will shove all usurpers from their chairs, by electrifying mankind with the right tone, long wished for, never heard. The true centre appearing, all false centres are suddenly superseded, and grass grows in the Capitol.

# MEMORY — PART II

*March 3, 1871*

◥

THE MIND, BY MEMORY, HAS AN INCESSANT PRESERVING AND accumulating power. The Past has a new value every moment to the active mind, through the incessant purification and better method of its memory. Once it joined its facts by color and form and sensuous relations; now it unites by intrinsic, natural,—and later, by spiritual relations. Some fact that had a childish significance to your childhood and was a type in the nursery, when riper intelligence recalls it, means more and serves you better as an illustration, and perhaps in your age has new meaning.

Memory was called *vespertina cognitio*; and Imagination, *matutina cognitio*. Memory is stability of knowledge. It is the victory of mind over time. The poet Dryden said, "Not Heaven itself upon the past has power," but we say, Memory has; and holds that slippery Proteus. When the Sophist offered for a price to teach him how to remember whatever he wished, Themistocles replied that he would give him twice so much money if he could teach him to forget. But this is only wit, and not reason. The body is the impediment; the body is the river of Lethe; its continual flowing and change is the cause of oblivion.

And to this purpose, method. The ordinary mnemonics, such as rhymes, are of undoubted use; every one has found himself helped by such. Thus the stranger in the city of Philadelphia is always helped by the rhyme to remember the order of the old streets,

> Chestnut, Walnut, Spruce, and Pine,
> Arch, and Mulberry, Race, and Vine.

Many men cannot recall the succession of the zodiacal signs without the almanac rhyme,

> The Ram, the Bull, the heavenly Twins,
> And next the Crab, the Lion shines,
> The Virgin, and the Scales,
> The Scorpion, Archer, and Hegoat,
> The man that holds the waterpot,
> And Fish with glittering scales.

These statements dishonor the mind. Tis a mechanic's view. The mind has a better secret in generalization, than in mere adding units to its list of facts. The experience and the thoughts of the past have a new value every moment to the advancing mind. What was an isolated belief or conjecture, our later experience instructs us how to place in just connection with other views which confirm and expand it. The old whim or perception was an augury of a broader insight, at which we arrive later with securer conviction. Thus all the facts in this chest of memory are property at interest.

Every faculty casts itself into an art, and that of memory into the art of writing, that is, the Book. It makes the difference of power between the soliloquy or the occasional remark of any man, and the power this gives him of selecting and combining the best thoughts of a lifetime. Tis the difference between the force of a single day, and that of 10,000 days; between the force of a single soldier, and a column of the army. For the daily thought trickles only drop by drop,—each sentiment or perception absorbing the mind, at the moment, to the exclusion of every other. But the memory holds every one of these intuitions—our own and other—in its firm grasp, and, on reflection, they throw themselves—like to like—into natural order, and he lives a new and enlarged being,—his heart beats with the blood of multitudes of men, and of many ages. Thus his convictions are not whimsical but cosmical. I value the praise of memory: and how does memory praise? Memory praises by holding fast the best. Plato remembered Anaxagoras by one of his sayings. If we recall our own favorites, we shall usually find that it is for one crowning act or thought that we hold them dear.

Do you not see what the mind is at this moment achieving in science—namely, finding the real links, always divined by great masters, but never made good by actual experiment and proof until now,—that each science repeats every other science in a common result, the *aliquid commune vinculum* which Cicero remarked, and which we now call *Correlation*, since Oersted and his compeers proved in fact that they were parallel before, and did not know it;

parallel, because each obeyed the same logic as each other one, since, as is now manifest, they were each a new disguise of one and the same force.

The damages of forgetting are more than compensated by the large values which new thoughts and knowledge give to what we already know. If new impressions sometimes efface old ones, see how in learning a new language every new word or phrase gained enlightens or strengthens what we have learned. I mean that, though in the multitude of new words, some earlier learned are overlaid and forgotten, yet we steadily gain insight into the genius of the language, the whole expanse is lighted up and each new particular word or phrase is more easily understood and kept.

Many attempts have been made to find means of strengthening a good memory, and of mending a bad one. Cicero tells us that Simonides invented the art of memory. "Lord Jeffrey had a fancy, or said that he had it, that, though he went to bed with his head stuffed and confused with the names and dates and other details of various causes, they were all in order in the morning,—which he accounted for, by saying, that, during sleep, they all crystallized round their proper centres." The vast choir of nature is grandly mnemonic, for every science repeats every other, and every new acquisition of thought lights up the old. Plato said, "That thing which is once well understood can never be altogether forgotten." Erasmus said after him, "The best art of memory is to understand things thoroughly,—and, being understood, to reduce them into order and, lastly, to repeat often what you would remember." Fulwood, in the *Castell of Memory*, says, "The soul must also be purged from evil things, that it may be filled with good things." And Marsilius Ficinus adds, "But besides those things that we have said, a perpetual sobriety of life doth most of all help."

It is certain that our own youth exerts an enormous influence through all our life. A most disproportionate part of our happiness comes from the recollection or restoring of its images and feelings. There is no poetry or sentiment, no love of beauty, which does not draw a charm from its retrospect or reminder of that magazine of good. Genius and virtue seem to be only a prolongation of that. Tis a little sad that we should always be spending on this patrimony, instead of multiplying a thousandfold our original stock.

It was a sublime-sounding fact which we used to hear of Egyptian temples, that the foundation stones showed carving on their undersides, showing that old as they were, they were ruins of an older civilization. And I found in Sicily that the church in Syracuse was an antique temple of Diana, but that was a mushroom to the Egyptian. And geology will show that first primaeval carved stone to have been a stratum precipitated and crystallized in what far aeons of uncounted time! Neither then were the particles and atoms new and raw, but mellowed and charred and decomposed from older mixtures,—when and where to reach their youth? A particle of azote or carbon, "nothing can in the least wear it." Well, the like *aerugo* sacred rust and smell of an immeasurable antiquity is on all with which we deal, or of which we are.

And the ruby bricks
Of the human blood
Have of old been wicks
In God's halls that stood

as Wilkinson huskily sings. Do we suppose it is newer with our thoughts? Do they come to us for the first time? These wandering stars and sparks of truth that shone for eternity and casually beamed this instant on us? The memory is made up of older memories: the blaze of genius owes its depth to our delighted recognition of the truth as something older than the oldest and which we knew aforetime, whether in the body or out of the body we cannot tell,—God knoweth.

The simple knot of *Now and Then* will give an immeasurable value to any sort of catalogue or journal kept with heed for a year or two. See in the merchant's counting room for peddling cotton and indigo, the value that comes to be attached to any blotting book or ledger; and if your aims and deeds are superior, how can any record of yours,—say, of the facts of life you would explain, of the books you would read, of the men you would measure,—any record you are genuinely moved to begin and continue,—not have a value proportionately superior at a later reading? It converts the heights you have reached into table-land. That book or fact which absorbed you a month ago, stands here along with one which was as vital in preceding months; and with that of yesterday,—and, next month, there will be another. Here they all occupy but a few lines, or pages, and you cannot read these together, without juster views of each, than when you recorded each singly.

A valuable property in memory is logic, or, the method by which its stores are arranged. This is the high difference;—the quality of the association by which a man remembers, whether by a trivial, or an essential trait,—by puns, or by principles. The moment I discover that this man observes and recalls—not by yellow string, or a knot in his handkerchief, or by reckoning from a pay-day, or by Gray's Mnemonics,—but by cause and effect, as the true geologist considers the strata from the axis of the globe, or the axis of nature, then, every word of his represents the harmony of the Kosmos, and I am as in the presence of Jove.

We are usually shut up in a short horizon of a few years. We do not originally remember anything beyond, say, seven years: beyond that term, only remember that we have remembered such a fact or story. It closes behind us,—our road,—for the eye of the mind, as of the body.

The memory plays a great part in settling the intellectual rank of men. A seneschal of Parnassus is Mnemosyne. Thus: have you found yourself a better scholar than one of your neighbors in the next block? You both have read the same books a year, two years, ten years ago. Both of you read the same new books of this month. Well, that fact which struck both of you then, with equal force, you still contemplate. He has lost it. He and the world have only the new fact of today: you have this and that other.

Then its values in the present. We remember what we use. We estimate a man not by what he has read, but by how much he remembers and uses. As the human stomach is not a mere sack, but an organic chemist, distributer and feeder of the whole body, so the memory is not a pocket or strongbox, but a living instructor, with a prophetic sense of the values which he guards.

The essence of memory being retentiveness, the perfection of it would be that it were absolutely tenacious, or that we should never forget anything. Niebuhr said, "I never forget anything that I have seen, read, or heard," and Steffens says of Humboldt, "Everything which he had learned was his forever."

All that we can say of thought is true of memory, the treasurer of thought. The retrospective value of a new thought is immense. Tis like a torch applied to a long train of powder. For the Memory is not dead but a living actor. And we may say of Memory what the Hindoo Upanishad says of the mind,—"Without hands and feet, he speeds, he takes; without eye he sees; without ear he hears; he knows all that is to be known, and yet there is none that knows him: the undecaying, ancient, the soul of all." The fact is fleeting and vanishes,—gone like a wreath of smoke. Tis only the thought or impression is taken up into the heaven of memory to endure.

And what are the limits of this faculty? There must be a proportion between the power of memory and the amount of knowledge, and, since the universe opens to us, the reach of the memory must be as large,—

> Eternal, boundless, undecayed,
> A thought unseen, but seeing all,

All, all in earth or skies displayed,
    Shall it survey, shall it recall:
Each fainter trace that memory holds
    So darkly of departed years,
In one broad glance the Soul beholds,
    And all that was at once appears.
Before creation peopled earth
    Its eye shall roll through chaos back;
And where the farthest heaven had birth,
    The spirit trace its rising track.
And where the future mars or makes,
    Its glance dilate o'er all to be,
While sun is quenched or system breaks,
    Fixed in its own eternity.

## 7

# INSPIRATION

*March 7, 1871*

◞

*By art, by music overthrilled,*
*The winecup shakes, the wine is spilled.*

PLUTARCH SAYS SOULS ARE NATURALLY ENDOWED WITH PRE-
diction. Dalton did not wait for empirical confirmation of his law
but promulged it, struck by its internal evidence. See the joy of
these seers in science,—when the famed lines Pythagoras devised
for which a hecatomb he sacrificed; or Archimedes, when bathing
in the water, the thought struck him how to find the alloy of the
gold in the crown, ran out into the streets naked; or Kepler's
haughty preface to his book: "I can well wait a hundred years for
a reader since God has been contented to wait 6,000 years for an
observer like myself." All the arts give the like testimony. "The first
sight of beautiful statues is to him who has feeling, like the first
view of the open sea, in which the eye is dazzled by its infinity but,
by repeated contemplation, the mind grows calmer and the eye
more steady, and we pass from the whole to the detail."

Expression is what he wants, not knowledge but vent; we
know enough, but have not leaves and lungs enough for a healthy

perspiration and growth. Hafiz has:  Hafiz's good things, like those of all good poets, are the cheap blessings of water, air, and fire,—the observations, analogies and felicities which arise so freely in writing a letter to a friend. An air of sterility,—poor, thin, reluctant vegetation,—belongs to the wise and the unwise whom I know. If they have fine traits, admirable properties, they have a palsied side. But an utterance whole, generous, sustained, equal, graduated at will, such as Montaigne, such as Beaumont and Fletcher so easily and habitually attain, I wish in myself most of all, but also in my contemporaries. A palace style of conversation, to which every morrow is a new day,—which exists ex tempore, and is equal to the needs of life,—at once tender and bold, and with great arteries like Cleopatra and Covinne,—would be satisfying, and we should be willing to die when our time came, having had our swing and gratification. But my fine souls are cautious and canny, and wish to unite Corinth with Connecticut. I see no easy help for it. Our virtues too are in conspiracy against grandeur, and are narrowing. The true nobility has floodgates,—an equal inlet and outgo.

When we remember how easily and happily we think in certain company, as, for instance, in former years with Alcott and Charles Newcomb,—earlier with B.P. Hunt,—though I must look far and wide for the persons and conditions, which yet were real,—and how unfavorable my daily habits and solitude are for this success, and consider also how essential this commerce is to fruitfulness in writing,—I see that I cannot exaggerate its importance among the resources of inspiration. There is an advantage of being somewhat *in the chair* of the company,—a little older and better-read, if one is aiming at searching thought. And yet how heartily I could sit silent, purely listening and receptive beside a rich mind.

Sit down to write with weak eyes, and your genius, when it wakes, will make them strong. Wisdom is like electricity. There is no permanent wise man, but men capable of wisdom, who, being put into certain company, or other favorable conditions, become wise for a short time, as glasses rubbed acquire power for a while. Every man is entitled to be measured or characterized by his best influence. Every loafer knows the way to the rum shop, but every angel does not know the way to his nectar:  why can we never learn our proper economy? Every youth and maid should know the road to prophecy, as surely as the cookmaid to the baker's shop.

The difference between labor and indolence in the world of thought certainly points at a code and scale of reward as emphatic as the Christian heaven and hell. Yet with this difference, that Inspiration is very coy and capricious. We must lose many days to gain one, and, in order to win infallible verdicts from the inner mind, we must indulge and humor it in every way, and not too exactly harness and task it.

Every dream even adds less stock to knowledge than it apprises me of admirable uses to which what I know may be turned. We know vastly more than we can digest. A strange dream: pyrotechnic exhibition of architectural or grotesque flourishes that indicate magazines of talent and invention in our structure, which I shall not arrive at the control of in my time, but tis my coat of arms, tis my blood-name, my peculiarity; and perhaps my great grandson will mature and bring it to the day.

Much may be done by timing your turns. Does today's problem require delicacy, self-possession or the flower of the mind? See to it overnight that pen and paper are ready, the inkhorn full, the room clean,—that no morning time need to be frittered on trifles that untune.

There is a beatitude of the intellect, a certain primary perception of truth which is too agitating for feeble souls. The wineglass shakes and the wine is spilled. There are to be sure certain risks about it as in the use of ether or alcohol. Aristotle said, "No great genius was ever without some mixture of madness, nor can anything grand and superior to the voice of common mortals be spoken, except by the agitated soul." Hence the value of some men of irregular genius. Wordsworth says of William Blake, "There is something in the madness of this man that interests me more than the sanity of Lord Byron and Walter Scott."

John Hunter one hundred years ago gave an important word to science, "arrested development," showing that the metamorphosis which in the lower kinds is arrested for ages,—in the perfecter, proceeds rapidly in the same individual. Well, there is the analogous power in the individual mind. Thought in the dull mind is rare and imperfect: in happy moments it is reinforced and carries out what were broken suggestions to larger scope and to clear and great conclusions.

Happy beyond the common lot if he learn the secret, that

besides the energy of his conscious intellect, his intellect is capable of new energy by abandonment to a higher influence; or, besides his privacy of power as an individual man, there is a great Public Power on which he can draw—by only letting himself go—by a certain abandonment to it—shall I say, by unlocking at all risks his human doors, and suffering the inundation of the ethereal tides to roll and circulate through him. This ecstasy the old philosophers called an inebriation, and said, that Intellect by its relation to what is prior to Intellect is a god.

Nothing can be done except by inspiration. The man's insight and power are local; he can see and do this, but it helps him not beyond; he is fain to make that ulterior step by mechanical means. It cannot be done. That ulterior step is to be also by inspiration;—if not through him, then through another man. Every real conquest is by "lyrical glances," by lyrical felicity, and never by main strength and ignorance. Years of mechanics will only seem to do it; it will not be done. "Neither by sea nor by land shall thou find the way to the Hyperboreans," said Pindar. We poorly strive by dint of time and hoarding grain on grain to substitute labor for the afflatus of Inspiration. Genius has not only thoughts, but the copula that joins them is also a thought.

The advantage we find in writing to a friend, the added genius we gain from affection, is a true inspiration. Novelty, surprise, changing of scene and subject refresh the artist, break up the tiresome old roof of heaven into new forms. In proportion to the force of the thought, the language is lifted. From poetry a large portion of the language is carefully excluded; only picturesque and sonorous words are used; but under a powerful thought every word of language is put into the poetical vocabulary, can be used as a word of heaven.

There's a sound healthy universe; the sky has not lost its azure because our eyes are sick. How we love to be magnetized! Ah, yes, strong iron currents take us in also. We are apologetic, such waifs and straws,—ducking, and imitating, and then the mighty current comes pouring on a silent wind, and fills us also with its virtue, and we stand like Atlas on our legs to uphold the world. Everything which we hear for the first time was expected by the mind: the newest discovery was expected. Inspiration is like yeast; many ways of getting it,—anyway gotten, you may apply it equally well to your purpose of making the bread. Tis the most difficult of tasks to keep heights which the soul is competent to gain.

In domestic labor or in task work for bread, the hearing of poetry or some intellectual suggestion brings instant penitence: the thoughts revert to the Muse, and under that high invitation, we think we will throw up our chore, and attempt once more this purer, loftier service. But if we obey this suggestion, the beaming goddess presently hides her face in clouds again. We have not learned the law of the mind, cannot control and bring at will or domesticate the high states of contemplation and continuous thought. "Neither by sea nor by land," says Pindar, "canst thou find the way to the Hyperboreans."—Neither by idle wishing nor by rule of three, nor rule of thumb.

Our philosophy is to wait. We have retreated in patience, transferring our oft-shattered hope how often to a larger and remoter good. We meant well, but were continually forced to postpone our best action, and that which was life to do, could only be smuggled into odd moments of the months and year. But we learn to say at last, Dear God, the life of man is not by man,—it is consentaneous and far-related: it came with the sun and nature; it is crescive and vegetative, and it is with us as it is with the sun and the grass. We obey the beautiful necessity. The powers that man wants will be supplied, as man is supplied, and the philosophy of waiting is sustained by all the oracles of the universe.

# COMMON SENSE

*March 10, 1871*

～

*In our domestic architecture is often a deficiency of light.*

COMMON SENSE IS PRIMARILY APPLIED TO THE CLEAR PERCEP-
tion of material objects, to distinguish sharply one from another,
and the qualities of each, so to know their use; then to persons and
duties, to language, numbers, proportion, facts, and thoughts. It
implies primarily a just dealing with persons and things according
to their natures. But in the young child it is already compounded
with affection, thought, and imagination. The child loves, hates,
resists and offends, idealizes his horse or doll, treats it as if alive,
and fables about it, dismissing his own common sense for the joy
of the imagination. Common sense is the accepting of the order of
nature as immutable, the man himself being a creature of shifting
moods. It respects therefore in its ordinary use the sensible world,
the common facts of human life.

Let us be just to this power and see its results. England now
for centuries has been its seat. England and the English race, and

now France and Germany; England which has put a new face on the world with its trade; which has colonized continents, and now in America, having planted itself like a banian anew in the ground, is growing with a bigger stock and sucking the juices of a continent which is a third of the world, to reproduce and extend its laws and institutions. The like vigorous scions grow in India, in Australia, in Africa, and carry the language round the globe. See iron roads clamping the farthest tracts of these huge continents and bringing all the rest of this magic of scientific machinery in their train. See French science, exact, pitiless, with crucible and chemic test and calculus in hand, traveling into all nooks and islands to weigh, to analyze and report. See the downfall of cant and nonsense; the fierce questioning and reduction to absurdity of every hoary abuse; the explosion of corn laws, the attack on Slavery, on Popery, on absolutism in every form. See the fruitful crop of social reforms,—Peace, Liberty, Labor, Health, Love, Churches of the Poor, Rights of Women.

Now a master mind must always have this direct eye to the material fact. No power of reasoning or of imagination or of virtue can excuse to men his want of it. He may be an angelical doctor, but he is not a man of this world. And men of grand genius have always combined with it this regulator. Socrates, Aristotle, Luther, Shakespeare, Newton, Franklin had it in large measure.

Coleridge's theory of Don Quixote is, that he is a man in whom the Reason, the great central moral and intellectual power, is sound and active, but the common sense wanting, so that he does not see facts as they are, but poetically, as in a dream, whilst Sancho Panza is the Common Sense embodied and is always right about them, and always defers to his master on the higher law. An ounce of mother wit is worth a pound of clergy. The part of the riding master is not to teach the boy to hold his reins prettily, but to sit like a jackanapes: never off. See too the good sense of Mr. Rarey, who taught England and America the true theory of taming and educating the horse.

In architecture, a house wants a good hat and a good pair of shoes. But if you look critically at a good many fine city houses, you will see that the chief conveniences are sacrificed to some piece of ostentation, as for instance the central drawing room in numberless blocks in New York and Philadelphia has no windows, but the light must be borrowed from the front or the rear apartment during the day,—or the chambers pay dear for a showy piazza,—or the chimneys are ill-constructed, and the eyes are tortured by smoke,—or the cellar is filled with water. If I have a haunted house, I don't call in a priest to sprinkle holy water, but I rent it to the editor of the village newspaper. If we are pestered with rats, we do not send for a conjuror: we put a cat in the pantry.

Idea and execution are not often entrusted to one hand. I was assured in the far West that the first planter, the leader of emigration to a township, was not commonly a successful man. Twenty or thirty years later he was not a large owner, but others who followed him, as if the impatience that made him the first continued to disqualify him from knowing when he was well off,—kept him changing, and therefore poor. There is an incompatibility of good speculation and good practice. Robert Owen, who founded New Harmony in Ohio and earlier his mills and gardens at New Lanark, is an example. His schemes were to cover England and America with New Harmonies, but he lived and died alone in his opinion.

"No people have true common sense but those who are born in England." Ah hapless! "When the simple nation like the Celt, the most imaginative finds itself face-to-face with the nation the most proud of its good sense!" Ireland goes to the wall. You must see the superb pity of English criticism surveying the fables on fables of Hindostan and Ireland.

Hunger, thirst, frost, night, disease, debt—what disagreeable but what indispensable masters are they to our education! If the contemplative life were practicable, to what subtleties and dreams would it not lead! What Laputas and schoolmen! The hot climate of India, and the vegetable food of the Gentoos, make it more possible, and hence the exaggeration of the Maia in all their theology,—which seems to the Saxon reader incredible as a dogma preached to a nation of men such as we are. Poverty, famine, ice, rain and rheumatism are the beadles and guardsmen that hold us to the common sense.

No scholar, be sure, listens without a certain envy to the running conversation of merchants at a boarding house, at their social address, coolness, and easy encounter, and their fluency and dexterity in helping themselves by so many lucky conventional phrases, newly-coined, perhaps, but sprightly, and giving life and humor to their story. Their conversation indicates that they see a crowd of people every day, know what the whole street is thinking about, and are too much accustomed to deal with many, to have any embarrassment in meeting one.

## 9

# WIT AND HUMOR

*March 14, 1871*

~

*A supreme beauty of wit is that you hear it at its birth.*

COMMON PEOPLE IN COMMON HOURS SEE EACH OBJECT PRE-sented to the mind, whether it be natural or spiritual, only in a partial way. They see it as it affects their wants or hopes or fears, but only some one side at a time. But each object has innumerable relations. And the difference of men is in the speed with which they discover these other relations. Wit is a sudden perception of all sides of the subject,—of relations so unexpected, and yet real, that we hear it with a pleased wonder that the speaker should see so fast and so truly. Speed is an essential trait of wit. The sculptor Thorwaldsden's remark, that "The clay was the life, plaster the death, and marble the resurrection of sculpture," is so accurately true, and yet apparently so accidental description of that art that it delights whilst it satisfies the mind. We say that "true wit never made us laugh." Fontenelle's remark, "I hate war, for it spoils conversation," is deeply true. Hadebras says, "Laws have no force till they are broken." The saying of the Greek Evenus at table was that "Fire is the best sauce."

"After my interview with Schelling, I went to hear Fichte lecture, who was just commencing his course on the constitution of man. His style of speech was cutting as a knife; his sentences fell like strokes from a razor. He took all possible pains to substantiate what he said by proof. 'Gentlemen,' he said, 'Withdraw within yourselves; enter into your own mind. We are now not dealing with anything outward, purely with ourselves.' The hearers, thus bidden, seemed really to withdraw into their own minds. Some changed their position and straightened themselves up; others bowed themselves over and closed their eyes. All waited with eagerness to see what should come next. 'Gentlemen,' continued Fichte, 'let your thought be the wall.' I could see that the hearers set their minds most intently upon the wall, and everything seemed favorable thus far. 'Have you thought the wall?' asked Fichte. 'Now then, Gentlemen, let your thought be, *that which thought the wall.*' It was curious to see what confusion and perplexity now seemed to arise. Many of the hearers seemed nowise able to discover that which had thought the wall, and I now understood how it might well happen that young men who stumbled over the first approaches to speculative philosophy in so clumsy a way, might in later efforts fall into errors which should be grave, if not dangerous. Fichte's lecture was exceedingly distinct and clear. I was wholly absorbed in his subject and had to confess that I had never listened to such a speaker before."

Sheridan's constituents were shoe-makers, and when he stopped in a journey at the town, one of them addressed him and complained that he had not remembered their interest in a measure before the Parliament,—Sheridan replied, "The devil take your trade! I wish it may be trodden underfoot by all the world." Haydon says, Jeffrey told me a story of Talleyrand at a public dinner in London. His health was drunk. Before the noise of approbation was over, he got up,—made a mumbling as if speaking,—spoke nothing, made a bow, and sat down; at which the applause redoubled, though all those immediately about him knew he never said a word. Napoleon asked, "What does all this negotiating about non-intervention mean? What is non-intervention?"—"Sire," said Talleyrand, "it signifies about the same thing as intervention." "Speech was given to man for the purpose of disguising his thought."

I once knew a man who was a perpetual holiday, and ought to be used like an oriflamme, or a garland for feasts and maydays, and parliaments of wit and love. When others were praised for their talents and concentration, he said he "had immense dispersive power." "Life is so short," he said, "that I should think that everybody would steal." There was a worthy farmer of our acquaintance rather given to grumbling and dark views of life. My friend told him that he "did not see but trouble was as good as anything else, if you only have enough of it." When question was of what disease a poor Irish laborer had died at the next farmer's house, he said "that he died of too much perspiration." And in another case, when of the sickness of our schoolmaster, opinions being various as to what the sickness was, he "thought his disease was a paralysis of talent." When a young gentleman's drawings were turned over, he remarked, "Yes, I think he would draw very well, if he had any talent for it." When the Massachusetts Life Insurance tables were made up by Mr. Bowditch, my friend said, if he was Mr. Bowditch, he would never insure any life that had any infirmity of goodness in it. We had a man named Winton in the town, who had passed a term in the state's prison. Now said my friend, "It is Winton who will catch pickerel: if he had any moral traits, he'd never get a bite." His literary opinions were quite as much his own. The merit of Irving's *Life of Goldsmith*, that he has not had the egotism to put in a single new sentence: Tis an agreeable repetition of Boswell, Johnson, and that company. And Montaigne is good, because there's nothing that has not already been *cured* in books, a good book being a Damascus blade made by welding old nails and horseshoes. Everything has seen service, and had wear and tear of the world for centuries, and now the article is brand new. So Pope had but one good line, and that he got from Dryden; and therefore Pope is the best and only readable English poet.

Humor is one of the most volatile of human expressions, and the most difficult to gather up and record, whilst it is pleasing and delightful in its momentary play. It needs a photographic memory in its companion, or is lost forever.

The one thing odious to us is joking. What can the brave and strong genius of Carlyle himself avail. What can his praise,—what can his blame avail me, when I know that if I fall, or if I rise, there still awaits me the inevitable joke? The day's Englishman must have his joke as duly as his bread. Heaven grant me the noble companions whom I have left at Rome who value merriment less and virtues and strengths more. If the English people have owed to their House of Commons this unmanning derision, I think they have paid an over-price for their liberties and empire. And when I balance the attractions of good and evil, when I consider what facilities, what talents a little vice would furnish,—then rise before me not these laughers, but the dear and comely forms of honor and genius and piety, in my distant home; they touch me with chaste palms moist and cold, and say to me the old words of Pythagoras, "Remember to be sober, and to be disposed to believe, for these are the nerves of wisdom."

Life has so many shadows in its day, so many vexations and regrets, so much gloom and dullness, that we need all our resources to keep it sweet. And mental activity is essential to health; and one of our best medicines is the surprise of gay conversation, and the power which some companions possess of diverting our thoughts from the shades and astonishing us by giving to somber and even gloomy facts a cheerful and even rejoicing face.

A plain strong man in France said to me of one of these wits "that what was intolerable to him was the twist that was in everything he said; and that he had just now heard from him more reasonable words than ever before, for, in talking with an American, he would leave his London out of the conversation." The London twist consists in inverting the common sense and experience of mankind on any and every subject, and affirming the reverse. My friend perceived no change in our party after they met in Paris, except that they had lost ground in speaking French. The Duke of Buckingham wished the dog who bit him a young wife and an estate in the country. And an eminent scholar whom I knew in London thought the only great, heroic and suffering man in Europe was the Czar Nicholas. But I remembered that our brave Thoreau at home used to complain that "the woods in winter are sultry." It is rather a cheap secret, however, this inversion or per-version,—simply to surprise by the exact opposite of the common sense. As it was wittily said of the ex-Emperor of France, that he was so ingenious a liar, that you could not even get at the fact by taking the exact opposite of his statement.

Every fact has a possible comic side, and wit delights in showing that side to the opponent's largest merit. To Schelling's doctrine of absolute identity of all things, Schlegel said, "Yes, all cats are black in the dark." Here tis the violent effort of the mind to conceive the depth of Nature at which all things are one. Lord Harvey's opinion was asked concerning a villa lately built by an acquaintance; he replied that "it was too small for a house, and too large to hang at your buttonhole." Wit never baulks at size or custom which bound the common mind.

# GENIUS

*March 17, 1871*

❦

*In proportion to a man's ideality, all objects have
    equal value.
The symbol always stimulates: therefore is poetry the
    best reading.*

GENIUS IS A DELICATE SENSIBILITY TO THE LAWS OF THE
world, adding the power to express them again in some new form.
When you say, "The times, the persons are prosaic; where is the feudal, or the Saracenic, or the Egyptian architecture? Where the
Romantic manners? Where the Papal or the Calvinistic religion,
which made a poetry in the air for Milton or Byron or Belzoni?
Our surroundings are as barren as a dry goods shop;"—you expose
your atheism. Is a railroad or a shoe factory or an insurance office,
a bank or a bakery outside of the system and connection of things,
or further from God, than is a sheep-pasture or a clam-bank? Is
chemistry suspended? Do not the electricities and the imponderable influences play, with all their magical undulations?

"Yet soon the conversation took a higher turn. In such
grandeur of nature, in such sense of freedom from all restraint of
convention, the nobler man unlocks willingly his inner mind, and

is ashamed to hold before himself the close mask of indifference, which, in daily life, is used to hold back the intrusive crowd. So also our Goethe! He from whom so rarely a decisive word on the holiest and gravest concern of humanity could be drawn, spoke this time of religion, moral culture, and the highest aim of the state, with a clearness and warmth such as we had never found in him in equal degree. The means of ennobling every thing sensuous, and to animate also the deadest facts through uniting them to the idea, he said, is the finest privilege of our supersensuous origin. Man, how much soever the earth draws him, with its thousand and myriad appearances, lifts yet a searching, longing look to the heaven which vaults over him in immeasurable spaces, whilst he feels deeply in himself that he is a citizen of that spiritual kingdom, our belief in which we must not repel or surrender. In this longing lies the secret of the eternal striving after an unknown aim. It is also the lever of our searching and thinking,—the soft bond between poetry and reality."

Genius is not personal, it is human, the Apotheosis of Man. Socrates. Michel Angelo. Newton. Jesus. Pascal. It lies close to Being. The superiority of the man is in the simplicity of his thought, that he has no obstruction, but looks straight at the pure fact with no colored opinion, so that compared with him, other people appear to be walking in a fog. The genius has the gentleness and simple manners and direct speech of childhood, far from the assumptions of public favorites. It does not cost him to see better than they, and he has might by his mere reality and gentleness. Parmenides thought the peculiarity of divine souls to consist in their being younger and at the same time older than themselves and other things.

Talent costs exertion: does something. Genius is. He cannot help his power and never needs to see to the proper recognition of his dignity. The greatest men impress by their presence, by their being. The people fell back from Jesus—they who would have resisted him if he had made defense. High genius is always moral: probity is its ground, and even DeQuincey,—not a very clear-sighted critic in this direction,—said, "Genius is talent—impregnated by moral sentiment."

> True bard and simple, as the race
> Of heaven-born poets always are,
> When stooping from their starry place,
> They're children near, though gods afar.

Burns was a man of genius, and with whatever frivolity spotted, had this clear humanity and natural religion, which made it easy for him, amid whatever trivialities, to recover himself, and say the simplest and noblest thoughts in language that cottages and palaces could equally accept. John Brown and Abraham Lincoln were both men of genius, and have obtained this simple grandeur of utterance. The surprises which genius has for us are in the homeliness of the fact, and the large scope or fruitfulness of the thought. Any path, every path, leads through Nature. A generalization may be made from every fact truly seen. How we value in children silent tenacity of their thought among the frivolous mates who are only eyes, and forget every moment the last object in the new.

Society is made up of men of talents. That which sleeps in them is Genius, and the use of metaphysics is in every way to lay bare this fact, and if possible awake this slumberer, and subordinate these too proud and busy hands to the god. Talent creates an artificial position with noise, but the gun can defend nothing but itself. But genius flings itself on elemental things which are powers—self-defensive;—which subsist and resist unweariably forevermore. Genius loves truth, and clings to it, so that what it does and says is not on a by-road, but on the great highways of nature which were before the Appian was built and will long outlast it.

The eye of genius looks through to the causal thought. Whilst the world of men give undivided heed to fact, Genius has been startled by perceiving the fact to be a mask, and detecting eyes that peer through it to meet its own. It knows that facts are not ultimates. Common sense stops at a fact; to it a fact is sacred: it will not go behind this, and it reckons mad those who do.

Genius unsettles everything. It is fixed, is it?—that after the reflective age has set in, there can be no quite rustic, original and united man born? Yes, quite rightly it belongs to all: it is a reception from the Pure Intellect,—a ray from *that* on the world in which we live,—this time not corrupted by the impurity of eye on which it falls. Day by day, hour by hour, men live as if crazed by the activity of the senses. Their experience is of a succession of trifles, of phantasms which oppress them, please and displease;—and they rarely retire from the gay or gloomy show to real Being, the white light, from whence what reason they have came.

This rare recurrence to the mind is the source of what sanity we have. Some minds are more open; and there are minds so simple, or so protected, that they easily receive truth from it. This is genius, the consoler of our mortal condition, the source of religion:

> Eyes that the beam celestial view
> Which evermore makes all things new.

Talent is a lower limitary skill, some knack. Intellect never again seems as before: for the state of *Being*, which is always divinely new,—ever flowing from its ineffable fountain,—is a condition of each experience. Thus Genius, like good generals, carries his base with him. Its trait is a negligence of yesterday's values, in its absolute confidence in the Eternal prompter.

# DEMONOLOGY

*March 21, 1871*

❧

THE NAME DEMONOLOGY COVERS DREAMS, OMENS, COINCI-
dences, luck, sortilege, magic, and other experiences which shun
rather than court inquiry, and deserve notice chiefly because every
man has usually in a lifetime two or three hints in this kind which
are specially impressive to him. They also shed light on our
structure.

The witchcraft of sleep divides with truth the empire of our
lives. This necromancer visits two children lying locked in each
other's arms, and carries them asunder by wide spaces of land and
sea, and wide intervals of time.

> There lies a sleeping city. God of dreams,
> What an unreal and fantastic world
> Is going on below!
> Within the sweep of yon encircling wall,
> How many a large creation of the night,
> Wide wilderness, and mountain, rock and sea,
> Peopled—with busy transitory groups,
> Finds room to rise, and never feels the crowd.

Tis superfluous to think of the dreams of multitudes,—the astonishment remains, that *one* should dream; that we should resign so quietly this deifying reason, and become the theatre of delirious shows, wherein time, space, persons, cities, animals, should dance before us in merry and mad confusion. Sometimes the gravest secrets of thought are told; sometimes the forgotten companions of childhood reappear.

> They come, in dim procession led,
> The cold, the faithless, and the dead,
> As warm each hand, each heart as gay,
> As if they parted yesterday.

A delicate creation outdoing the prime and flower of actual nature, antic comedy alternating with horrid pictures. We seem busied for hours and days in peregrinatings over seas and lands, in earnest dialogues, strenuous actions for nothings and absurdities, cheated by spectral jokes, and waking suddenly with ghastly laughter to be rebuked by the cold, lonely, silent midnight, and raking with confusion in memory among the gibbering nonsense, to find the motive of this contemptible cachinnation. Meantime, this limbo and dust-hole of thought is presided over by a certain reason, too. We know ourselves in this mad crowd, and owe to sleep and dreams a certain divination.

The foremost trait of the dream is a dislocation. A painful imperfection belongs to them. Fairest forms and agreeable scenes are disfigured by some pitiful insane circumstance. The very landscape and scenery in dreams seem not to fit us, but, like a cloak or coat of some other person, overlap and encumber the wearer; so is the ground, the road, the house, in dreams, too long or too short, and quite too mutable, and serves at least to show us how accurately nature fits man awake.

In speaking, the other day, of memory I noticed that we remember some things in one mood which we forget in another. In like manner, there is one memory of waking, and another of sleep. In our dreams, the same scenes and fancies are many times associated, and that, too, it would seem, for years. One shall meet a whole crew of boarders at some dream-house, of which gentlemen and ladies we can trace no remembrance in any waking acquaintance. In sleep he shall travel certain roads in coaches or gigs, which he recognizes as familiar, and has dreamed that ride a dozen times; or shall walk alone in field or meadow,—which road or which meadow in waking hours, he never looked upon. This feature of dreams deserves the more attention from its resemblance to that obscure startling experience which almost every person confesses in daylight, that particular passages of conversation and action have occurred to him in the same order before, whether dreaming or waking—that he has sat with precisely these persons in precisely this dialogue, at some former hour, he knows not when.

Another trait in dreams is that they have their own Fauna. Animals have been called "the dreams of nature." Perhaps, we go to our dreams for a conception of their consciousness. In a dream we have the same instinctive obedience, the same torpidity of the highest power, the same unsurprised assent to the monstrous as these metamorphosed men exhibit. Our thoughts in a stable or in a menagerie, on the other hand, may well remind us of our dreams. What compassion do these imprisoning forms awaken! You may catch the glance of a dog sometimes, which lays a kind of claim to sympathy and brotherhood. What! somewhat of me down there? Does he know it? Can he too, as I, go out of himself,—see himself,—perceive relations? We fear lest the poor brute should gain one dreadful glimpse of his condition, should learn in some moment the tough limitations of this pinched organization. It was in this glance that Ovid got the hint of his Metamorphoses, Calidasa of his transmigration of souls,—for these fables are our own thought carried out. What keeps those wild tales in circulation thousands of years? What but the wild fact to which they suggest some approximation of theory? Even in varieties of our own species, where organization predominates over the genius of man, in Kalmuck, or Bushman, or Papuan, we are pained by the same feeling, and sometimes the sharp-witted, prosperous white man awakens the like. You think, could he overlook his condition, he could not be held from suicide.

Dreams have a poetic integrity and truth. Their extravagance from nature is yet within a higher nature. They are like monstrous formations, (for example, the toes that occasionally show themselves in a horse's hoof), and denote the generic law. Wise and sometimes terrible hints shall in them be thrown to the man, out of a quite unknown intelligence. He shall be startled two or three times in his life by the justice as well as the significance of the intimations of this phantasmagorica. Once or twice the normal bonds of the spirit shall be unlocked, and a freer utterance gained. Dreams pique us by independence of us. My dreams are not me; neither are they nature, or the *not me*; they have a double consciousness, at once sub- and ob-jective. I call the phantoms that rise the creation of my fancy, but they act like mutineers and fire on their commander, showing that every act, thought, and cause is bipolar, and in the act is contained the counteraction. If I strike, I am struck: if I chase, I am pursued.

A prophetic character haunts them. Our dreams show like the sequel of waking knowledge. The visions of the night bear some kindred to the visions of the day. Actions whose turpitude is very differently reputed proceed from one and the same affection. Sleep takes off the costume of circumstance, arms us with a terrible freedom, so that every will rushes to a deed.

Dreams, however monstrous and grotesque their apparitions, have a substantial truth. The like is true of omens, coincidences, presentiments, which sometimes astonish. The reason of the appearance is latent in the life of the individual. Why should not symptoms, auguries, forebodings be, and the moanings of the spirit?

The soul contains in itself the event that shall presently befall it, for the event is only the actualizing of its thoughts. "A man's destiny is his temper." More truly, a man's fortune is in his character. Tis no wonder then if the affairs in which he engages, the words spoken by him and to him, the events that befall, should in a marked manner express his character and the legitimate issues of that character. Tis no wonder that particular dreams, omens and coincidences should be prophetic, because all are prophetic. The fallacy consists in selecting a few insignificant passages when all are steeped in the same sense.

Every man goes attended by innumerable facts prefiguring his fate,—if only eyes of sufficient penetration were fastened on the sign. The sign is there, if only the keen observer were also; just as, under every tree in the speckled sunshine and shade no man notices that every spot of light is a perfect image of the sun, until in some hour, the moon eclipses the luminary, and then first we notice that the spots of light have become crescents or annular, and correspond with the changed figure of the sun. Things are significant enough, Heaven knows, but where is the seer of the sign? No doubt, a man's fortune may be read in the lines of his right hand by palmistry, in the lines of his face by physiognomy, in the outlines of the skull by craniology. The lines are all there,—could you only find a reader who knew the cipher.

The long waves indicate to the mariner that there is no near land in the direction from which they come. Belzoni describes the three marks which led him to dig for a door to the pyramid of Ghizeh. What thousands had stood in the same spot, through so many ages, and had seen no three marks. All life, all creation is tell-tale and betraying. A man reveals himself in every glance, and step, and movement and rest.

"Head with foot hath private amity,
And both with moons and tides."

Not a mathematic axiom, but is a moral rule. The jest and byword (to an intelligent ear) extends its meaning to the soul and to all time. All that proceeds from man is so anthropomorphous that not possibly can the poet invent any fable that shall not have a deep moral and be true in senses, and to an extent, never thought of by the inventor. The idlest fables of Homer and Ovid, modern philosophers explain of law, of state, and ethics. Lucian's tale that Panerates journeying from Memphis to Coppus and wanting a servant, took a door-bar and pronounced over it some magical words, and it stood up and brought him water, turned a spit, and carried bundles, doing all the work of a slave. Is this a prophecy of our industrial arts? For Panarates read Arkwright, Fulton, or Watt, and for magical words, read loom or steam, and do they not make an iron bar or piston do the work, not of one, but of a thousand skilful mechanics? Secret analogies tie together the remotest parts of nature, as the atmosphere of a summer morning is filled with gossamer threads running in every direction, but revealed by the beams of the rising sun.

In times most credulous of these whimsies, the sense was recognized and the superstition rebuked. When Hector is told that the omens are unpropitious, he replies, "One omen is good, to die for one's country." And Lucan writes in the same spirit, "Dire is the omen when the valiant fear." Euripides said, "He is not the best prophet who guesses well, and he is not the wisest man whose guess turns out well in the event, but he, who, whatever the event be, takes reason, and probability for his guide." "Swans, horses, dogs, and dragons," says Plutarch, "we distinguish as sacred and vehicles of the divine foresight, and yet we cannot believe that men are sacred, and favorites of heaven." The poor shipmaster discovered a true theology, when, in the storm at sea, he made his prayer to Neptune, "O God, thou mayest save me if thou wilt, and, if thou wilt, thou mayest destroy me, but, however, I will steer my rudder true."

The belief that particular individuals are attended by a good fortune, which makes them desirable associates in any enterprise of uncertain success, exists not only among those who take part in political and military projects, but in all joint action of commerce and affairs. A corresponding assurance exists in the individuals so distinguished, who justify the expectation of others by a boundless self-trust. "I have a lucky hand, sir," said Napoleon to his hesitating chancellor; "Those on whom I lay it are fit for anything." This faith is familiar in one form, that often a certain abdication of prudence and foresight is an element of success, that children and young persons come off safe from casualties that would have proved dangerous to wiser people. We do not think the youth will be forsaken; but he is fast approaching the age when the sub-miraculous external protection is withdrawn, and he is committed to his own care. The young man takes a leap in the dark, and alights safe. As he comes into manhood, he remembers passages and persons that seem, as he looks at them now, to have been supernaturally deprived of injurious influence on him. His eyes were holden that he could not see. But he learns that such risks he may no longer run. He observes with pain, not that he incurs mishaps here and there, but that his genius, whose invisible benevolence was tower and shield to him, is not longer present and active.

In the belief of men, ghosts are a selecting tribe, avoiding millions, speaking to one. In our traditions, fairies, angels, and saints show the like favoritism; so do the agents and the means of magic, as magicians and amulets. This faith in a doting power, so easily sliding into the popular belief everywhere, and, in the particular of lucky days and fortunate persons, as frequent in America today as the faith in incantations and philtres was in old Rome, or the wholesome potency of the sign of the cross in modern Rome;— This supposed power runs athwart the recognized powers, natural and moral, which science and religion explore. Heeded though it be in many actions and partnerships, it is not the power to which we build churches; or make liturgies and prayers; or regard in passing laws; or found college professorships to expound the science of. It is a different nature and habit. Walter Scott, that Doctor of Demonology, makes the White Lady reply to the monk's inquiry, Who and what she is?

> That which is neither ill nor well,
> That which neither stood nor fell,
> A wreath of mist, a bubble of the stream,
> Twixt a waking thought, and a sleeping dream,
> A form that men spy
> With the half-shut eye,
> In the beams of the setting sun, am I.

It would be easy in the political history of every time to furnish examples of this irregular success, men having a force which, without virtue and without shining talent, yet makes them prevailing. No equal appears in the field against them. A force goes out from them which draws all men and events into their favor. The crimes they commit, the exposures that follow and which would ruin any other party, are strangely overlooked or do more strangely turn to their advantage. Lies and truths, crimes and blunders, equally turn to their account.

I set down these things as I find them, but however poetic these twilights of thought, I like daylight, and I find somewhat willful, some play at blindman's buff, when wise men talk of the demonological. The insinuation is that the known eternal laws of morals and of matter are sometimes corrupted or eluded by this gypsy principle, which chooses favorites, and works in the dark for their behoof; as if the laws of the Father of the Universe were sometimes baulked and eluded by a meddlesome Aunt of the Universe for her pets.

You will observe that this extends the popular idea of success to the very gods:  that they foster a success to you which is not a success to all; that fortunate men, fortunate youths exist, whose good is not virtue, or the public good, but a private good robbed from the rest. Tis a midsummer madness, corrupting all who hold the tenet. The demonologic is only a fine name for egotism, an exaggeration, namely, of the individual whom it is nature's settled purpose to postpone. The race never dies; the individual is never spared. Great men feel that they are so by sacrificing their selfishness and falling back on what is humane; in renouncing family, town, clan, country, each exclusive and local connexion, to beat with the pulse and breathe with the lungs of nations. A highland chief, an Indian sachem, or a feudal baron may fancy the mountains and lakes were made specially for him, Donald, or for him, Tecumseh: that the one question for history is the pedigree of his house, and future ages shall be busy with his renown. He has a Guardian Angel; he is not in the roll of common men; obeys a high family destiny; when he acts, unheard of success evinces the presence of rare agents. What is to befall him, omens and coincidences foreshow: when he dies, banshees will announce his fate to the kinsmen in foreign parts. What more facile, than to project this exuberant selfhood into the region where the individuality is forever bounded by generic and cosmical laws? The popular religious creeds tend to intrude the same element of a limited personality into the high place which nothing but spiritual energy can fill, introducing names and persons where a will is an intrusion,—into growth, repentance, and reformation.

We may make great eyes, if we like, and say of one on whom the sun shines, "What luck presides over him!" But we know that the law of the universe is one for each and for all. There is as precise and as describable a reason for every fact occurring to him as for any occurring to any man; every fact in which the moral elements intermingle is not the less under the dominion of fatal law than the properties of light, or water, or salt, or sugar. Lord Bacon

uncovers the magic when he says, "Manifest virtues procure repu-
tation; occult ones, fortune." Thus the so-called fortunate man is
one who, though not gifted to speak when the people listen or to
act with grace or with understanding to great ends, yet is one who
in actions of a low or common pitch relies on his instincts, and simply does not act where he should not, but waits his time, and
without effort acts when the need is so that in a particular circle
and knot of affairs he is not so much his own man, as the hand of
nature and of time; whereas the fault of most men is that they are
busy-bodies,—do not wait the simple movements of the soul, but
interfere and thwart the instructions of their own minds. If to this
you add a fitness to the society around him, you have the elements
of fortune.

The history of man is a series of conspiracies to win from
nature some advantage without paying for it. Tis curious to see
what grand powers we have a hint of, and are mad to praise, yet
how slow Heaven is to trust us with such edge-tools!

Mesmerism is high life below stairs, or Themus playing Jove
in the kitchens of Olympus. Tis a low curiosity or lust of structure,
and is separated by celestial diameters from the love of spiritual
truth. There are many things of which a wise man might wish to be
ignorant, and this is one of them. Shun them as you would the
secrets of the undertaker, of the butcher. These adepts have mis-
taken flatulency for inspiration. Were this drivel which they report
as the voice of spirits really such, we must find out a more decisive
suicide. I say to the table rapper,

'I well believe
Thou wilt not utter what thou dost not know,
And so far will I trust thee, gentle Kate.'

They are ignorant of all that is healthy and useful to know, and by law of kind,—dunces seeking dunces in the dark of what they call the spiritual world,—preferring snores and gastric noises to the voice of any muse. I think the rappings a new test, like blue litmus, or other chemical absorbent, to try catechisms with. It detects organic skepticism in the very heads of the Church. The triviality of information I obtain from these mesmerized is, that, pain is very unpleasing; that my shoes are made of leather; that the cock crows in the morning; and that there is a great deal of water in the seas. But the real objection to spiritism is that it is in the wrong hands. New powers are certainly to be looked for. Who has found the limits of human intelligence? Yes, they are to be looked for, but not in the ignorant nor in the immoral. And Bettine said that "the reason spirits so seldom appear is that they do not like phantoms, ugly phantoms, such as men are."

# Transcendency of Poetry

*March 24, 1871*

❧

WE ARE SOMETIMES APPRISED THAT THERE IS A MENTAL power and creation more excellent than anything which is commonly called philosophy and literature; that the high poets,—that Homer, Milton, Shakespeare, do not fully content us. How rarely they offer us the heavenly bread! The most they have done is to intoxicate us once and again with its taste. They have touched this heaven, and retain afterwards some sparkle of it. They betray their belief that such discourse is possible. There is something,—our brothers on this or on that side of the sea do not know it, or own it,—the eminent scholars of England, historians, and reviewers— romancers and poets included—might deny and blaspheme it,—which is setting us and them aside, and the whole world also,—and planting itself.

To true poetry we shall sit down as the result and justification of the age in which it appears, and think lightly of histories and statutes:—none of your parlor or piano verse,—none of your carpet poets, who are content to amuse, will satisfy us. Is not poetry the little chamber in the brain where is generated the explosive force, which, by gentle shocks, sets in action the intellectual world? Bring us the bards who shall sing all our old ideas out of our heads, and new ones in: men-making poets,—poetry, which, like the verses inscribed on Balder's Columns in Briedablik, is capable of restoring the dead to life:—poetry like that verse of Saadi, which the angels testified "met the approbation of Allah in the Heaven;"—poetry which finds its rhymes and cadences in the rhymes and iterations of nature, and is the gift to men of new images and symbols, each one the ensign and oracle of an age! That shall assimilate men to it,—mould itself into religions and mythologies, and impart its quality to centuries,—poetry, which tastes the world, and reports of it, upbuilding the world again the thought:

> "Not with tickling rhymes,
> But high and noble matter, such as flies
> From brains entranced, and filled with ecstasies."

Poetry must be affirmation. It is the piety of the intellect. *"Thus saith the Lord"* should begin the song. Landon's opinion is "that it is reserved for a better state of existence and sensation."

The poet who shall use nature as his hieroglyphic must have an adequate message to convey thereby. Therefore, when we speak of the Poet in any high sense, we are driven to such examples as Zoraster and Plato, Isaiah, St John, and Menu, with their moral burdens. The Muse should be the counter-part of Nature, and equally rich. I find her not often in books. We know Nature, and figure her exuberant, tranquil, magnificent in her fertility, coherent, so that every creation is omen of every other. She is not proud of the sea, of the stars, of space, or time, or man, or woman. All her kinds share the attributes of the selectest extremes. But in current literature I do not find her. Literature warps away from life, though at first it seems to bind it. In the world of letters how few commanding oracles! Homer did what he could,—Pindar, Aeschylus, and the Greek Gnomic poets, and the tragedians. Dante was faithful when not carried away by his fierce hatreds. But in so many alcoves of English poetry, I can count only nine or ten authors who are still inspirers and lawgivers to their race.

It is not style or rhymes or a new image more or less that imparts, but sanity; that life should not be mean, that life should be an image in every part beautiful, that the old forgotten splendors of the Universe should glow again for us,—that we should lose our wit, but gain our reason, and when life is true to the poles of nature, the streams of truth will roll through us in song. To know the merit of Shakespeare, read *Faust*. I find Faust a little too modern and intelligible. We can find such a fabric at several mills, though a little inferior. *Faust* abounds in the disagreeable. The vice is prurient, learned Parisian. In the presence of Jove, Priapus may be allowed as an offset, but here he is an equal hero. The egotism, the wit is calculated. The book is undeniably written by a master, and stands unhappily related to the whole modern world; but it is a very disagreeable chapter of literature, and accuses the author, as well as the times. Shakespeare could, no doubt, have been disagreeable, had he less genius, and if ugliness had attracted him. In short, our English nature and genius has made us the worst critics of Goethe:

> "We, who speak the tongue
> That Shakespeare spake, the faith and manners hold
> Which Milton held."

I have heard that there is a hope which precedes and must precede all science of the visible or the invisible world; and, that science is the realization of that hope in either region. I count the genius of Swedenborg and Wordsworth as the agents of a reform in philosophy, the bringing poetry back to nature,—to the marrying of Nature and Mind,—undoing the old divorce in which poetry had been famished and false, and Nature had been suspected and pagan. Homer and Shakespeare had been true to both. The philosophy which a nation receives rules its religion, poetry, politics, arts, trades, and whole history.

A good poem,—say, Shakespeare's *Macbeth*, or *Hamlet*, or the *Tempest*,—goes about the world offering itself to reasonable men, who read it with joy, and carry it to their reasonable neighbors. Thus it draws to it the wise and generous souls, confirming their secret thoughts, and, through their sympathy, really publishing itself. It affects the character of its readers by formulating their opinions and feelings, and inevitably prompting their daily action. If they build ships, they write *"Ariel"* or *"Prospero"* or *"Ophelia"* on the ship's stern, and impart a tenderness and mystery to matters of fact. The ballad and romance work on the hearts of boys who recite the rhymes to their hoops, or their skates if alone,—and these heroic songs or lines are remembered, and determine many practical choices which they make later. Do you think Burns has had no influence on the life of men and women in Scotland, has opened no eyes and ears to the face of Nature, and the dignity of man, and the charm and excellence of woman?

We are a little civil, it must be owned, to Homer and Aeschylus, to Dante and Shakespeare, and give them the benefit of the largest interpretation. We must be a little strict also, and ask, whether, if we sit down at home, and do not go to Hamlet, Hamlet will come to us? Whether we shall find our tragedy written in his,—our hopes, wants, pains, disgraces, described to the life,—and the way opened to the paradise which ever in the best hours beckons us?

Much that we call poetry is but polite verse. The high poetry which shall thrill and agitate mankind, restore youth and health, dissipate the dreams under which men reel and stagger, and bring in the new thoughts,—the sanity and heroic aims of nations,—is deeper hid, and longer postponed than was America, or Australia, or the finding of steam, or of the galvanic battery.

In a cotillion, some persons dance, and others await their turn when the music and the figure comes to them. In the dance of God, there is not one of the chorus but can and will begin to spin,—monumental as he now looks,—whenever the music and the figure reach his place and duty. O celestial Bacchus! drive them mad,—this multitude of vagabonds, hungry for eloquence, hungry for poetry, starving for symbols, perishing for want of electricity to vitalize this too much pasture, and, in the long delay, indemnifying themselves with the false wine of alcohol, of politics, or of money.

The poet is rare because he must be exquisitely vital and sympathetic, and, at the same time, immovably centered. In good society, nay, among the angels in heaven, is not everything spoken in fine parable, and not servilely as it befell to the sense? All is symbolized. Facts are not foreign as they seem, but related. Wait a little, and we see the return of the remote hyperbolic curve.

The solid men complain that the idealist leaves out the fundamental facts; the poet complains that the solid men leave out the sky. To every plant there are two powers; one shoots down as rootlet, and one upward as tree. You must have eyes of science to see in the seed its nodes; you must have the vivacity of the poet to perceive in the thought its futurities.

The Poet is representative,—whole man, diamond-merchant, symbolizer, emancipator: in him the world projects a scribe's hand and writes the adequate genesis. The nature of things is flowing, or metamorphosis. The free spirit sympathizes not only with the actual form but with the power or possible forms: but for obvious municipal or parietal uses, God has given us a bias or a rest on today's forms. Hence the shudder of joy with which in each clear moment we recognize the metamorphosis, because it is always a conquest, a surprise from the heart of things.

Every man may be, and at some time a man is lifted to a platform whence he looks beyond sense to moral and spiritual truth;— and in that mood deals sovereignly with matter, and strings worlds like beads upon his thought. The success with which this is done can alone determine how genuine is the inspiration.

One would say of the force in the works of nature: All depends on the battery. If it give one shock, we shall get to the fish form, and stop; if two shocks, to the bird; if three, to the quadruped; if four, to the man. Power of generalizing differences men. The number of successive saltations the nimble thought can make, measures the difference between the highest and lowest of mankind. The habit of saliency,—of not pausing but going on,—is a sort of importation and domestication of the Divine effort in a man. After the largest circle has been drawn, a larger can be drawn around it.

The problem of the poet is to unite freedom with precision; to give the pleasure of color, and be not less the most powerful of sculptors. Music seems to you sufficient, or the subtle and delicate scent of lavender; but Dante was free imagination,—all wings,— yet he wrote like Euclid; and mark the equality of Shakespeare to the comic, the tender and sweet, and to the grand, and terrible.

A little more or less skill in whistling is of no account. See those weary pentameter tales of Dryden and others. Turnpike is one thing and blue sky another. Let the poet of all men stop with the inspiration. I much prefer the opposite whim of Goethe, in affecting the commonplace, as if he would persuade you that his balloon was the county-jail.

We must not conclude against poetry from the defects of poets. They are in our experience men of every degree of skill,—some of them only once or twice receivers of an inspiration, and frequently falling back on a low life. The drop of *ichor* that tingles in their veins has not yet refined their blood, and cannot lift the whole man to the digestion and function of ichor,—that is, to god-like nature. Time will be when ichor shall be their blood,—when what are now glimpses and aspirations shall be the routine of the day. Yet even partial ascents to poetry and ideas are forerunners, and announce the dawn. In the mire of the sensual life, their religion,—even their superstitions, their poets, their admiration of heroes and benefactors, their novel, their newspaper, even, are hosts of ideals,—a cordage of ropes that hold them up out of the mire. Poetry is inestimable as a lonely faith, a lonely protest in the uproar of atheism.

I hate to read such expressions as that of Dr. Johnson concerning Milton, "Our language sunk under him and was unequal to the greatness of soul which furnished him with such glorious conceptions." The first way in which a great mind shows its power, is, in making language. Milton could do justice to his thought. If Milton could not, Shakespeare could. The language would serve God, if he would. Strong thinking makes strong language: correct thinking, correct speech.

People wonder sometimes that persons uneducated to write, should be able to use language with purity and force. But the manner of using language is a decisive test of intellectual power, and he who has force can hardly conceal it therein. For speech is the first and simplest vehicle of mind,—is of all things next to the mind; and the vigorous Saxon who uses it well, is of the same block,—*adamas ex veteri rupe,*†—as the vigorous Saxon that formed it, and works after the same manner.

Tis the property of symbols to delight. The poetic theory is the generation of matter from thought. Plato and Swedenborg are the expounders of the doctrine. The moralists, like Zeno, and Socrates, and Jesus, and Buddha, and Confucius, are the didactic poets. But so many men are ill-born or ill-bred,—the brains are so marred, so imperfectly formed, unheroically—brains of the sons of fallen men,—that the doctrine is imperfectly received. Psychology is fragmentarily taught. One man sees a spark or shimmer of the truth, and reports it, and his saying becomes a legend or golden proverb for ages, and other men report as much, but none wholly and well. Poems,—we have no poem. Whenever that angel shall be organized and appear on earth, the Iliad will be reckoned a poor ballad grinding.

I doubt never the riches of nature, the gifts of the future, the immense wealth of the mind. O yes, poets we shall have,—mythology, symbols, religion, of our own. We too shall know how to take up all this industry and empire, this Western civilization into thought, as easily as men did when arts were few;—but not by holding it highly, but by holding it low. The intellect uses, and is

---

† Out of the same ancient rock

not used,—uses London and Paris and Berlin, East and West, to its end. The only heart that can help us is one that draws, not from our society, but from itself, a counterpoise to society. What if we find partiality and meanness in us? The grandeur of our life exists in spite of us,—all over and under and within us, in what of us is inevitable and above our control. Men are facts as well as persons, and the involuntary part of their life so much as to fill the mind, and leave them no countenance to say aught of what is so trivial as their selfish thinking and doing. Sooner or later, that which is now life shall be poetry, and every fair and manly trait shall add a richer strain to the song.

Our over-praise and idealization of famous masters is not in its origin a poor Boswellism, but an impatience of mediocrity. We ought not, and shall not be contented with any goal we have reached. What we call greatness today, is only such in our bar-barous or infant experience. Every saint, every poet, every man comes one day to be superfluous. How fast we outgrow the books of the nursery,—then those that satisfied our youth! Better not to be easily pleased. The poet should rejoice if he has taught us to despise his song;—if he has so moved us as to lift us; to open the eye of the intellect to see farther and better.

## 13

# Laws of Mind

### *March 28, 1871*

⌐

Thought is identical, the oceanic one which flows hither and thither and sees that all are its offspring, and coins itself indifferently into house or inhabitant, into planet, man, fish, oak, or grain of sand. All are reconvertible: every atom is saturated with it and will celebrate in its destiny the same laws. Every thing by being comes to see and to know. Work is eyes, and the artist informs himself in efforming matter.

As a Kentuckian cannot see a man without wishing to try a fall with him and break his back over an iron bannister, so there are men who cannot see the sun or stars without the wish to wrestle with them. Here is Descartes, Kepler, Newton, Linnaeus, Swedenborg, LaPlace, Schelling, who will wrestle with the problem of genesis and construct cosmogonies. Nature is saturated with deity. The particle is saturated with the elixir of the universe. Little men just born copernicise. They cannot radiate as suns and revolve as planets, and so they do it in effigy by building their orrery in their brain.

Philosophy seeks to find a foundation in thought for everything which exists in fact.

*Diderot*: If there is not a God perhaps there will be one.

I will not push this objection further. Tis only a difference of more and less. I also value the introspection when it aims at use, when it is guided by genius or natural skill.

*Above*: Tis only more and less.

Above the thought is the higher truth—truth as yet undomesticated, and therefore unformulated. Is there not somewhat surgical in metaphysics as we treat it. Were not an ode a better form. I think there must be a moral charm to all beauty, and if you take the moral sentiment out of your catalogue of powers, the catalogue loses truth and the right to our attention and only such a list of powers or history of power can interest me as is itself derived from enjoyment of the powers in their action. We must have approached and seen the gods we describe, Mnemosyne and her nine Muses, Apollo, Themis, Hermes, Jove, the celestial Venus, the Graces, the Parcae, Nemesis, and these rightly seen by the true bard will have none of the ill features which loose poets have added, but only eternal beauty and attributes of the human consciousness.

There are times, (and these are the memorable hours of life,) when that vault is full of light, when a man finds the world in his own mind, when he sees that outward nature and art and history have their beginnings here,—have their origin in his thought. The mind is eternal and abides;—these pass away.

But how shall this beatitude be described to science? "All difference is quantitative." Every law of nature is only a translation of every other law. Every law of matter is only a pictorial representation of a law of mind. The reason why Imagination finds types everywhere in nature is because chemistry or astronomy or zoology all only externize the laws of the mind. Twenty men (each full of some thought different from all the others) find confirmation and analogy for their several aims in the same experiments. The youth delights in the novelty of each object in turn, but, by and by, he discovers, like the Greek philosopher Xenophanes, that things are imposters, or that each novelty is an imposter and only covers the selfsame familiar experience;—he was tired of the same old song, and wished to die. It is true that perception reacts on the organs it employs. We value our national acuteness. But better men have been and can be. Was it Atkinson, the English traveller, who found in Northern Asia people of such perfection of organ that they could see the satellites of Jupiter with the naked eye? And the Greek historian tells us, that the Athenians could see the temple of Minerva at Aegina twenty-three miles away. Tis certain that we can sooner see an object for the mind's knowing it is there: better for knowing the nature, form, and position of the object, as in the familiar example of an old seaman looking out for land in approaching a well-known coast. The patient naturalist finds at last the process he is looking for.

And as mind, our mind, or mind like ours, reappears to us in our study of nature,—nature being everywhere formed after a method which we can well understand, and all the parts, to the most remote allied and explicable,—therefore our own organization is a perpetual key, and a well-ordered mind brings to the study of every new fact or class of facts a certain divination of that which he shall find. Newton said, "The world was made at one cast." The doctrine of Identity is the last generalization. To the child all appears difference; but later he classifies things which resemble outwardly or inwardly one another. Gradually he finds these resemblances and makes new classification and at last sees what vast identity exists throughout: that every form is parallel with every other; that the laws of each class of beings correspond to the laws of another, and of every other; the laws of the body correspond to those of the mind. But this is a late process. Men are in their thoughts and cannot order them, cannot detach them. Later the man of genius detaches them, compares them, sees their likeness or unlikeness, ranks them, sees that these are above him and others are outgrown, are below him, comes to generalize, as we say, or see that many of his experiences are all examples of one law: he lays up that law in his memory and drops the thousand facts.

Well, having well accepted this law of identity pervading the universe, we next perceive that whilst every creature represents and obeys it, there is diversity more or less of power; there is high and low; that the lowest only means incipient form, and over it is a higher class in which its rudiments are opened, raised to higher powers; that there is development from less to more, from lower to superior function, and *that* steadily ascending to man. Ascension of state is the next law—in the least egg to complete maturity; and in the next higher animal to maturity also; up to man, and in man from the child to the adult; from the savage to the Greek, and from the slave to the freeman; from the unwise to the wise and virtuous. And none so able or so high, but all his accomplishment is only a perception of interminable knowledge and power existing yet unattained before him. Tis indifferent whether you say, All is matter or All is spirit; and tis plain, there is a tendency in the times to an identity philosophy. You do not degrade man by saying, Spirit is only finer body; not exalt him by saying, Matter is phenomenal merely. All rests on the affection of the theorist,—on the question, whether his aim be noble. Here and there were souls which saw through banquets and wine, lands, offices, money, and vulgar pleasure,—saw that these as objects of desire were all alike and all cheats,—perish in the using. But the soul is distinguished by its aim,—what is the end? This re-acts, this far future consummation which it seeks—re-acts through ages and ennobles and illuminates every passing moment, consecrates the individual among his coevals, though they had every advantage of skill, force, and favor. Here and there is a soul which is a seed or principle of good,—a needle pointing to the true north,—thrown into the mountains of foolishness and deserts of evil, and therefore maligned and isolated by the rest. This soul has the secret of power; this soul achieves somewhat new and beautiful which endears heaven and earth to mankind and lends a domestic grace to the sun and the stars.

It is one of the remarkable signs,—I do not know but the

most remarkable sign of the times,—the "fascination which facts, superficially considered the strongholds of materialism, are beginning to exert on the minds which have the least sympathy with a low materialism." I do not know that I should feel threatened or insulted if the chemist should take his protoplasm or should mix his hydrogen, oxygen, and carbon and make a plant or an animalcule incontestably swimming and jumping before my eyes. I might feel that the day had arrived when the human race might be trusted with a new degree of power, and its immense responsibility, for these steps are not solitary or local, but only a hint of an advanced frontier supported by an advancing race behind it. What at first scares the spiritualist in the experiments of natural science, as if thought were only finer chyle,—fine to aroma,—now redounds to the credit of matter, which, it appears, is impregnated with thought and heaven and is really of God and not of the devil, as he had too hastily believed. All is resolved into unity again. My chemistry, he will say, was blind and barbarous,—but my intuition is, was, and will be true. It is the unexpected triumph of Idealism.

Science is concentrating in our time. The scattered hints of so many students each experimenting on one region of Nature answer to each other like rhymes or like translations of the same book into different languages,—or, shall I say, like the finding in the Norse and the German and the Persian and the Indian traditions the same identical fables and nursery tales. The languages of many nations, of almost all nations, are found to be dialects of one tongue. The modern words are found to be only disguises of the same primaeval roots; the arts to be only adaptations of the same principles to the varying exigences of different climates and local materials. The gods of each religion can be identified in every other by a corresponding deity, as the Zeus of Greece with Jove at Rome, Hermes with Mercury, Athene with Minerva, Bacchus with Liber, the Eumenides with the Parcae, Artemis with Diana. The parallelism of magnetic attraction with that of electricity is at last found to be identical, and has opened the deeper generalization of the convertibility of all the grand agencies of light, heat, chemical affinity, magnetism, gravity into one principle. In animal life the like system and secret fundamental unity is conceded, and the wildest variety of form and function explains itself everywhere as gradations of one harmonious whole. There are no monsters. Nothing in man is anomalous. All is orderly and his reason now contemplates and affirms that he finds this order and fitness. Then he finds that there are more harmonies than these,—namely, that the world of matter replies to the mind; that every thought of his mind has a representation in outward nature; and that he cannot clearly conceive and formulate his thought but by indicating some fact in nature, as if to say, I perceive clearly, he should say, I have the sun in my mind; I am melancholy, Tis all night in me. All words are originally names of material objects.

Nature through all her works makes one silent demand of man; it is thus: Be master. "I will finish the house," she says; "Be you the tenant; not a piece of the furniture, but the lord and user of all. Be thou the mighty benefactor. Don't be scared by size: only fools are. What are millions of leagues, what are dreary durations to thee? Suns and atoms, tis all the same. An atom is all. One atom is like another, and a sun is nothing but a larger lump of the same atoms. Every breath of air is a carrier of the soul of the world. And when once thy mind knows the law of so much as thine own body, thou hast nothing to learn from galaxies of stars. Tis not diameters, but ideas and insights that make depth and vastness. Ponderable and imponderable agents that work through wild space are only extensions of thy hands and feet."

# METRES OF MIND

*March 31, 1871*

❧

*"That which sees is itself the thing which is seen."*
—*Plotinus*

BUT THERE IS A METRE WHICH DETERMINES THE CONSTRUC-tive power of men,—this, namely, the question whether the mind possess the control of its thoughts, or they of it. The new sect stands for certain thoughts. We go to individual members for an exposi-tion of theirs: vain expectation. They are possessed by the ideas, but do not possess them. One meets contemplative men who dwell in a certain feeling and delight which are intellectual, but wholly above their expression. They cannot formulate. They impress those who know them by their loyalty to the truth they worship, but can-not impart: saints too. George Fox has hardly left a readable page. His records are for the most part groanings that cannot be uttered. I have seen the like in the worshippers of philosophy and literature. Wordsworth calls his brother a silent poet. Sometimes the patience and love are rewarded in life by the chamber of power being at last opened, but sometimes they pass away dumb, to find it where all obstruction is removed.

The ability of men or of a period is estimated by the depth of the ideas from which they live, and to which, of course, they appeal. "The most manifest sign of wisdom is a continual cheerfulness." Life is incessant parturition. None of these masters we are continually citing is so great but finds one who apprehends him. Nay, no historical person begins to content us; and this is a pledge of a higher height than he has reached, and in our meditation on the problems of Nature and the mind, when we have arrived at the question, the answer is already near.

We are to each other results. As my perception or sensibility is exalted, I see the genesis of your action and of your thought; I see you in your cleft and fountains, and to my eye, instead of a little pond of life, you are a rivulet fed by rills from every plain and height in nature, and antiquity, and deriving a remote origin from the source of things.

There is an effect of time on every mind which appears like the vegetation. The mind in long periods does not acquire so much from abroad, as inveterate itself in its own quality. The effect of long life on any man is to make more pronounced that nature and quality he is.

There is a concentration of merits in every great work, which, though successive experiences in the mind of the master, were primarily combined in the piece. Therefore, we ought to come to a picture twenty times, in the light of twenty new views of man and nature. How many times, in the course of a year, we entertain a thought which puts a new face on all things! These are the chimes of our clock, announcing that we have lived into another hour. But this the master also had found; this divine realism, shattering the veils of the Apparent, he also had shared. We readily understand that his hand improved by familiarity with new styles, by practice, and so forth. But did his philosophy lay no color on the pallet, or exalt no form? We believe in his growing skill in technics of his art, in color grinding, chiaroscuro, and the rest. But the real difference between picture and picture is the age of thought in the painter's mind. We require this peculiarity in each: the opinions of men in general lose all worth to him who perceives that they are accurately predictable from the ground of their sect and party, and not proper to themselves.

In the Persian fables the divine horses refuse any rider but their own hero. A man might as easily mount a lion as to mount Kyrat, if Kyrat's master have not first laid the bridle on his hands. "Leonardo da Vinci thought but little," says Bossi, "of any general measure of the species, and held that the true proportion and the one most difficult of investigation is solely the proportion of an individual in regard to himself, which, according to the true imitation should be different in all the individuals of a species as is the case in nature." This determination of each man is from all the others, like that of each tree up into free space. The reliance on simple perception constitutes genius and heroism, and that is the religion before us. The act of perception instantly throws man on the party of the Eternal. The savant erects himself into a barrier, is not willing to report Nature—to stand by and report, but must report Nature

Cuvierized, or Owenized, or Blainvillcized, which modification diminishes the attraction of the thing in a fatal manner.

All thought is perception of truth. All truths are related, and the mind perceives this order and consent of parts throughout nature. All truth is practical, leads and impels to its embodiment or incarnation in facts and institutions. Then the best part of it is,—not the fruits or facts, not the profit—but the mind's part herein. Tis a lesson we daily learn in conversing with men that it is not so important what the topic or interest is about which we deal as is the angle of vision under which the object is seen:—that means, that it be seen in wide relations, seen with what belongs to it near and far, and the larger the mind the more truth. One man astonishes by the grandeur of his scope, another confines by the narrowness of his.

The talent sucks the substance of the man. How often we repeat the disappointment of inferring general ability from conspicuous particular ability. But the accumulation on one point has drained the trunk, and we cry, Blessed are those who have no talent. The expressors are the gods of the world,—Homer, Shakespeare, Goethe, and the rest; but the sane men, whom these expressors revere, are the solid, balanced undemonstrative minds, who make the reserved guard, the central sense of the world.

A master can formulate his thought. Our thoughts at first possess us. Later, if we have good heads, we come to possess them. The masters are exact minds, severe with themselves, and can formulate something. Can you formulate your dogma? They rush to

their solitude, lock themselves up as in a prison, that they may consider, and compare, and arrange these wild and flying thoughts, find
their true order; if it is the mind itself which they study, that they
may discover what is instinct, what is memory, what is imagination,
and fancy. What?—a horse doctor can give a prescription to cure a
horse's heel. Have you no recipe for a bad memory or a slow perception or a sick angel?

Tis because he is not well mixed, that he needs to do some
feat by way of fine or expiation. How rarely we meet a person superior to his talent!—like one who has money in his pocket, but
disdains to use it, being personally equal to all his needs. There
comes an orator excellent to melt all sorts of hearers into perfect
fusion for the time, and he does not inspire the smallest wish to
know anything of his mind; none for personal intercourse. Let him
value his talent as a door into nature; let him see his performances
only as limitations. Then over all let him value the sensibility that
receives, that loves, that dares, that affirms. Intellect detaches, yet
men of talent sometimes make fools of themselves by too much
detachment. A man came once to me in my study and introduced
himself, saying, "Sir, I wish to read you some papers. I am now for
six years devoted to the sun: I study the sun, that I may deduce the
laws of the human mind." I said I will not dispute against the sun,
but beware of taking anything out of its connections, for that way
madness lies; and I looked into his face to see if there insanity
shined.

But thus none can adhere but the men who are born of that

idea which they express. And every one can do his best thing easiest. Your own act is always cheerful to you: anybody else's in your hands is a bore to you. We talk of schools, but God makes one man of each kind. That makes the eternal interest of persons to each other. "My son cannot replace me: I could not replace myself: I am the child of Destiny," said Napoleon. I have heard it said by some persons that they always remember any one who interested them by his or her face as it appeared at their first acquaintance, and do not see the changes wrought by time. Be that as it may. How grateful is it to discover the new emphasis in each. Was not this bias a dainty invention, whereby the old worn world and every part and particle of it should be made wholly new material for you? Of course, each of us only partially comprehends the other because he is new and unlike us, and we hesitate about his eccentricity and his hobby. The air would rot without lightning; and without the violence of direction that men have,—without bigots, no excitement, no efficiency. And my belief is that each soul represents a certain fact in nature, a law, sometimes a fact in natural science or in political or in morals, a law of beauty, or of metaphysics, or of mechanic power whose demonstrator or orator he is and should be, that justice may be done to that particular fact among men. Thus opinions are organic. By this means, what power is conferred! In mechanics, the aim has continually been to obtain the perpetual push, instead of the spasmodic or alternated push; for example, the power of a running river to turn machinery, instead of the successive pulses of steam. The steady push in one direction is the differencing power of the man born with a ruling thought. Tis just the difference between travel by railroad and walking across broken country: immense speed, but can only go in one direction.

A strong nature feels itself brought into the world for its own development and not for the approbation of the public. We are glad of a day when we know what we are to do in it and of every day so long as we are obeying our true genius. Everything will come home, a man also. Where is his home? There, whither he is incessantly called. The new man—no history writes it as he knows it. His prudence, his charity are new. The greatest pride of a man consists therein, that the recognition of him by others is nowise necessary to him. *Reverere tibi*. Respect your thought. Who are you that you should desert it? Cato a monotone with his *Delenda est Carthago.*[†] Demosthenes a monotone, and Chatham, and John Adams, Bismark, and every other powerful person. I wish every man truly to please himself: then he will please me. If you surrender your individuality, you lose your strength and all real success. Niebuhr said, "A public infallibly lowers the tone of an author who descends to try to please it." Thus the politician who goes blindly for the platform of his party loses the interest of the wise minority in the public,—the minority, whose better opinion is sure to become the ruling opinion. Not less is this true in private circles. People interest us as long as there is some reserve about them. Only that mind draws me which I cannot entirely read. Tis just the same

---

† "Carthage must be destroyed"

with the public which you address. So long as your thought piques it with somewhat more than it can fully master, their curiosity and new attempting will not fail.

The universe and the Individual perpetually act and react on each other. Thus all philosophy begins from Nox and Chaos, the ground or abyss which Schelling celebrates. And in every man we require a bit of night, of chaos, of *abgrund*, as the spring of a watch turns best on a diamond. In every individual we require a *pièce de resistance*, a certain abyss of reliance and fortitude on which to fall back, when worst comes to worst. That continent, that backbone being secure, he may have what variety, what surface, what ornament or flourish he will. I do not think violent changes of opinion often occur in strong men. As far as I know, they do not often see new lights and turn sharp corners; but commonly, after twenty or after fifty years, you shall find the individual true to his earlier tendencies. Mahomet writes in the Koran, "If you hear that a mountain has changed its place, believe it: but if you hear that a man has changed his disposition, believe it not." The change is commonly in this wise,—that each becomes a more pronounced character; that he has thrown off those timidities and imitations which masked his own.

Bias: that instinct which guides the boy when his teachers misguide him. Couture, the French painter, has just shown us how indignantly his father resisted the boy's instinct and reckoned him a dunce. When the father at last yielded, how learnedly and systematically the Academy resisted, and almost crushed his native skill with their rules, till he was the worst painter in the school; only in secret and with the boys he avenged himself and out-painted all his masters. In the school he grew worse and worse, but out of school he copied nature and was a great painter. One day a head he had drawn of one of the boys was found by the master: "Who painted this head?"—"Couture." "Impossible," said the master, but it was his, and at last he was allowed to go his own great way. I once heard Professor Faraday deliver a lecture in the Royal Institution on Dia-magnetism, in which he explained to his audience that whilst iron and other substances, on being magnetized, tended to place themselves north and south,—nickel and other substances had a different polarity, and ranged themselves east and west; that gases and indeed every substance had its own polarity; and he proceeded to prove by experiment these surprising differences, and to show us that polarity was not a law of a few exceptional metals or textures, but a universal law. He did not carry his doctrine to any application beyond matter. But I find the extension into the history of mind easy, and inevitable into Intellect and into morals. Every soul has a bias or polarity of its own, and each new. Every one is a magnet with a new north; that every mind is different, and the more it is unfolded, the more pronounced is that difference.

And the height of culture, the highest behavior consists in the identification of the ego with the Universe, so that when a man says, I hope, I find, I think,—he might as properly say, the human race thinks, or finds, or hopes; he states a fact which commands the understandings and assents of all the company; and meantime, he shall be able continually to keep sight of his biographical ego, I have a desk, I have an office, I am hungry, I had an ague,—as rhetoric or offset to his grand spiritual ego, without impertinence, or ever confounding them. Therefore when one sees good men in any society where the rule is stringent, he is annoyed by the certain gène or crippling, as, for example, in the Shaker Society or the monastic orders or Masonic; he does not like the rule or society the better for the good man, but resents the rule: feels him to be disadvantaged just so far as the rule works on him.

# WILL

*April 3, 1871*

❧

ONE MEASURE OF MENTAL HEALTH IS THE DISPOSITION TO the affirmative to find good everywhere,—good, and order, analogy, health, and benefit,—the love of truth, tendency to be in the right, no fighter for victory, no cockerel. "Ascending souls sing paean." "The Lord gives, but never takes away."

There are two mischievous superstitions. I know not which does the most harm: one, that "I am wiser than you," and the other, that "you are wiser than I." The truth is that every man is furnished, if he will heed it, with wisdom necessary to steer his own boat if he will not look away from his own to see how his neighbor steers his.

Use your powers, and put them to the best use. Tis the used key which is bright. Those faculties will be sharp, which are employed,—imagination, reasoning, numbering, or fighting,—just as Indian legs are strong and arms are weak. Great affectation in all our mental science, as we call it. We are spectators, merely, and wonderers, when we are at our best,—when in happiest hours larger views or vistas are opened to us.

Freedom is a thing of degrees. Is a slaveholder free? Not one. Is a politician? Not one. See the snakes wriggle and wind! Is a man free whose conscience accuses his lies, thefts, indulgences, without number? Is he free whom I see, when my eyes are anointed, to be always egotist and blinded by his preference of himself? A humble man can see, but a proud man or a vain man is a patient for Dr. Eliot, the oculist. Jacobi maintains that he could instantly kill himself by certain metaphysical thoughts if he did not repel them, but should hold them fast. Seneca says of his sickness, "the thought of my father, who could not sustain such a blow as my death, restrained me,—I commanded myself to live." "If a man has only a will once for all, which goes through life, not alternating from minute to minute, from being to being,—that is the main thing." What inspiration in every assertion of the will! Thus I find a stimulus in the first proposition of political economy, "that all wealth is derived, not from land, but from labor." "I think there is some reason for questioning whether the body and the mind are not so proportioned that the one can bear all that can be inflicted on the other; whether virtue cannot stand as long as life, and whether a soul well-principled will not be separated sooner than subdued."

When a thought or an act commends itself to the intellect as true, and to the soul as good,—of wholesome effect,—we call it affirmative. What is useless or noxious we call negative. Thus the Greek and the Turkish doctrine of Fate is noxious. Now all teaching that shows the omnipotence of the will is spiritual,—of good effect; and never was anything gained by admitting the omnipotence of limitations. In politics an unjust preference of one citizen, or class of citizens, is negative action and will have mischievous results. Trace the colossal conceptions of Buddhism and Vedantism home, and they are the necessary or structural action of the human mind: Buddhism, the tenet of Fate; worship or morals, the tenet of Freedom,—the unalterable originals in all the wide variety of geography, language and intelligence of human tribes. "My experience is that men of great talents are apt to do nothing for want of vigor. Vigor, energy, resolution, firmness of purpose,—these carry the day. Is there one whom difficulties dishearten, who bends to the storm? He will do little. Is there one who will conquer? That kind of man never fails. Hunter the surgeon. Let it be your first study to teach the world that you are not wood and straw,—some iron in you." The primary rule for conduct of the intellect is to have control of the thoughts without losing their natural attitudes and action. They are the oracles: you shall not poke and drill and force but follow them. We believe that certain persons add to the common vision a certain degree of control over these states of mind; that the true scholar is one who has the power to stand beside his thoughts, or to hold off his thoughts at arm's length and give them perspective, to form *il piu nell uno*, the many in one. The spirits of the prophets are subject to the prophets.

We should no more complain of the obstructions which make success in poetry, oratory, art, or in character difficult, than we should complain of the iron walls of the gun which hinder the shot from scattering. It was walled round with iron tube with that intent, to give it irresistible force in one direction. We hate cheap successes. We like the victories of Columbus, of LaPlace, of George Stephenson, well-won, hard-earned, by fifty years of toil, and an invincible will. "Wisdom is not found in the hands of those who live at their ease." Life is so affirmative, that we cannot hear of personal vigor of any kind, great power of performance, without sympathy and fresh resolutions.

No hope is so bright but is the beginning of its own fulfillment. Believe in the beneficent unweariable power of Destiny. Belief consists in accepting the affirmations of the soul; unbelief in denying them. Pindar said, "A man doing good things forgets Hades." I think it a practical rule, this— Do not trust good news that comes to you, unless you can also give good news. Work on; you cannot escape your wages.

Books are worth reading that announce an affirmative thought. All others are comparatively tickings of a clock, and we have so much less time to live,—the robbers that they are. Especially every one hates doleful books. "In poetry, only the really great advances us." In thought, every generalization shows the way to a larger. There is an Eastern proverb, "No seed will die." Tragedy, as such,—a tale of struggle with a certainty of defeat and ruin,—is pure pain. Genius uses it only as a dark ground on which to paint with more glorious effect the grand resistance of the soul. Only as this is so treated as to leave the beholder fortified and uplifted by this triumphant affirmative is a tragedy fit ground for the poet. The

*Prometheus* (Aeschylus), the *Antigone* (Sophocles) of the Greeks accomplish this. So does Shakespeare in *Hamlet* and *Lear* and Walter Scott in the *Bride of Lammermoor*. But most tragedies are purely doleful. The question is,—in what frame of mind does it leave the reader or spectator?—in the despondent, or in the affirmative mood? Kant says, "the pleasure of eloquence and the fine arts arises from their power to drive off to a greater distance the limits of human destiny. The narrow bounds of earth disappear, when the glorious career of genius and virtue is opened to the mind."

# CONDUCT OF INTELLECT

*April 5, 1871*

❧

"*It is characteristic of entire sincerity to be able to foreknow.*"
"*The individual possessed of complete sincerity is like a spirit.*"
—*Confucius*

THE OUTWARD WORLD IS ALL ORGANIC AND NECESSITATED, to the last tract and hair. The inward is not less. There is an order in every mind. And it is because there is an order, that you can find it in the works of any particular artist. It requires a poetic mind to write commentaries on Aeschylus or Dante. The power of Linnaeus or of Oken to explain nature is that they are timed to it step for step; they come upon that they look for, or find it because they bring it with them. But not less excellent and ranking is the power to unfold instead of adding. The poet from the inception commands his complete fable. All the parts are organic and required, each from the first. But bad artists, when they begin, do not foresee the end, or what is to come next. Tis the difference between the Classic and Romantic schools. A great deal of denying, preparing, wondering, and quoting in literature, but of calm affirming very little. He makes me rich, him I call Plutus, who shows me that every man is mine and every faculty is mine; who does not impoverish me in praising Plato but adds thereby assets to my inventory. Profound sincerity is the only basis of talent, as of character. "Truth first." The temptation is to patronize Providence, to fall into the accepted ways of talking and acting of the good sort of people. But the virtue of the intellect is its own, its courage is of its own kind, and, at last, it will be justified, though for the moment it seem hostile to what it most reveres.

Bonaparte is a perpetual type and exemplar for an intellectual man. Bonaparte said to Bubna, the Austrian diplomatist in 1809, "My great advantage is in being constantly on the offensive with you, not only at large, but also in detail, and in every particular moment. I am not on the defensive, except when I do not see you,—for instance in the night,—but as soon as I see you, I resume the offensive. I form my plan, and I force you to fly my movements."

We need all our resources to live in the world which is to be used and decorated by us, and Socrates kept all his virtues as well as his faculties well in hand. He was sincerely humble, but he did not less know how to use his humility as a decoy to the unwary children of conceit, whom he allowed and humored in talking down to him until their fall was sure in the nets of his logic, and utilized his humility chiefly as a better eye-glass to penetrate the vapors that baffled the vision of other men. He was brave, but there was no soldiering in his witty intercourse with his daily companions.

But the first rule must be applied. The world exists for use.

Use the faculty, labor, drudge and wrestle for it. This kind cometh not but by practice, and prayer and fasting. Remember the grand counsel that came down from I know not what Chaldaean seer,— "To the persevering mortal the blessed immortals are swift."

Persevere, add stone to stone, build. It is much to record your results in sentences. Tis more to add method and report the spirit of your life symmetrically. Of those who read good books and converse about them, the greater part are content to say, I was pleased, or, I was displeased; it made me active, or inactive,—and rarely does one eliminate or define the quality of that life which the book woke in him. So rare is a general reflection. But to arrange many general reflections in their natural order, so that I shall have one homogeneous web, a "Lycidias," an "Allegro," a "Penseroso," a *Hamlet*, a *Midsummer's Night's Dream*, this continuity is for the great. The wonderful men are wonderful hereby. The observations that Pythagoras made respecting sound and music are not in themselves unusually acute, but he goes on, adds fact to fact in an order; makes two steps, three steps, or even four, and every additional step counts a thousand years to his fame.

I found all on the faith that is in man. The affirmative in us reaches from pole to pole, and there is no room for the negative. All life, all genius, all progress is that; the negative is sin and death. "If ye have faith as a grain of mustard seed, nothing shall be impossible to you."

Intellect detaches, yet the way men make fools of themselves is, by too much detachment. A man knocks at my door and says: I am now for six years devoted to the sun that I may deduce the laws of the universe. I say: I will not dispute against the sun, but beware of taking any one thing out of its connections, for that way folly lies. It is no matter how strong is your understanding or how rich your rhetoric; no book is good which is not written by the Instincts, no book in whose birth Fate and the Times had not a controlling influence. A fatal frost makes cheerless and undesirable every house in which animal heat is not. We yawn over cold allegories however elegant. See the advantage of a superior, simultaneous survey of all the kingdoms of nature. How different the attitude of Linnaeus, Cuvier, and Agassiz, from Leewenhoeck, Dr. Harris, and Prof. Peck. To these the comparison of tribes and kingdoms and the procession of structure in sunfish and mammal is open, whilst the others count the cilia and spines on a beetle wing.

"For a matter of this kind cannot be expressed by words, like other things to be learnt, but by a long intercourse with the subject, and living with it, a light is kindled on a sudden, as if from a leaping fire, and being engendered in the soul, feeds itself upon itself." The population of the globe has its origin in the aims which their existence is to serve. The truth takes flesh in forms that can express and execute it, and thus, in history, an idea overhangs like the moon, and rules the tide which rises simultaneously in all the souls of a generation. As the world is made of thickened light and arrested electricity, so ideas are the parents of men and things. They are the First Good, of which, Plato affirms, that "all things are for its sake, and it is the cause of everything beautiful." Now this light, this glory, like the corona which the astronomers have found around the sun, is real, and is the contribution of the mind; it is its announcement of the truth that is in nature, and which the beast and the savage do not see, but which advancing science is ever uncovering.

The spiritual determines the practical. Who can overestimate the power of Poetry? Every man is a poet, without knowing it. It governs every people. It makes carts, ships, railroads, wars, annexations. Men's thoughts and their sentiment determine all they do in all departments down to the most material. It has been said, "The thoughts they had were fathers of the actions they did, and their feelings were the fathers of their thought." Emotion is the first stage, thence thought, and thence action. Kant thought all the faculties of the soul may be reduced to three, which admitted not of being reduced to any other, Cognition, Emotion, and Will.

Now that surprise and delight which each child finds in his Being, and which animates and exaggerates to him every fact in turn, it is not easy to define or classify: it is both cognition and emotion, and it leads directly to will. It is a certain light or glory which invests and magnifies all objects which he beholds, and powerfully affects his will. See how in earnest the child is with his toys, and how imaginative! How real and serious his dealing with his wooden horse or toy house! How indignant if you treat it as a block, and not an enchanted creature. He is a poet. Well, his sentiment, his poetry goes on educating him. All strong feeling opens the eyes. The heart is delighted with nature, with the sea, the risks,—the power to conquer it,—the mystery of it. What else draws men to the passion for the sea? The boy makes his toy boat, and it floats; makes a rag into a sail, and it obeys the wind. Soon he gets into a real boat and trims a sail and feels a pure joy at making the wind serve him. It is an untold delight in nature and the celebration of it in songs and novels, that drives the youth to hunting, to war, to the sea-life, and to love.

> Much have I seen and known; cities of men
> And drunk delight of battle with my peers,
> Far on the ringing plains of windy Troy.
> Yet all experience is an arch wherethro'
> Gleams that untravell'd world, whose margin fades
> For ever and for ever when I move.
> Come, my friends,
> 'Tis not too late to seek a newer world.
> Push off, and sitting well in order smite
> The sounding furrows; for my purpose holds
> To sail beyond the sunset, and the baths
> Of all the western stars, until I die.
> It may be that the gulfs will wash us down:
> It may be we shall touch the Happy Isles,
> And see the great Achilles, whom we knew.
>
> —*Tennyson*

The youth has heard of distant countries across the sea, strange climates, strange fruits, strange men, in strange dress, strange dwellings, and his imagination is engaged to trade with such beings and things, instead of following some employment that has less charm for his imagination. But the boy near him who goes into some mechanic trade at home,—if his confessions were made, would have his little romance also to gild what seemed a prosaic choice. What made the Crusades, but that all Europe was filled with a poetic inspiration which united the races and nations for the first time, brought them together and created the manners and institutions of chivalry. So did the search for the fabulous India and El Dorado, afterwards, and Plymouth Colony, the Declaration of Independence, were the late results.

# RELATION OF INTELLECT AND MORALS

*April 7, 1871*

❧

THE SIMPLEST FORMS OF BOTANY, AS THE LICHENS, ARE ALIKE
all over the globe. The lichens of Sweden and Brazil and Massachusetts are the same, whilst in the more complex classes of the
flora, each zone and meridian has its own. So is it with the simple
and grand characters among men,—they do not hold of any nationality or of any catechism. So of the grand ideas of religion and
morals. Viasa and Pythagoras and Swedenborg see the same thing.
The grand, simple characters appear in one race as in another. Even
the French, weak in moral traits, have Malebranche, Montesquieu,
Pascal, Fenelon, Guion. These affinities destroy nationality. The
moral sentiment domesticates us at once with entire strangers.

Tis ever a strange fact that so many men of various talent,
including men of eminent special ability, do not recognize the
supreme value of character. In history we appreciate it fully. We all
read Plutarch or Tacitus with one mind; unanimously take sides
with Agesilaus in Sparta, with Aristides, Phocion, Demosthenes,
Socrates in Athens; with Epaminondas in Thebes, with Dion in

Sicily; and wonder that the Athenians should side with the Cleons, and Critiases, Meletus, Anytus, against these grave and noble persons. In Rome, we give our suffrages again for Regulus, Scipio, Paulus Aemilius, Cato, Trajan, Marcus Aurelius, against their profligate rivals. So, in England, we respect the names of Alfred, of Burke, Fox, Romilly, Wilberforce, Bright, Gladstone; in America, the purity and exceptional elevation of Washington.

In European history, Luther's conscience animating sympathetically the conscience of millions, the pulse passed into thought, and ultimated itself in Galileos, Keplers, Bacons, Cromwells and Miltons. Tauler, George Fox, Jacob Behmen, Madame Guion, Pascal,—persons of deep moral convictions, subordinating all intellectual culture to these, even holding intellect in a certain dislike as profane. Swedenborg, though a man of extraordinary science and culture, shared this feeling. And in almost every man's acquaintance there is probably some one example where the great sensibility of conscience has stood to the person in lieu of mental culture, and has strengthened the imagination, the memory, the insight in a wonderful manner. Herman Grimm in his history of Michel Angelo shows Michel, Vittoria Colonna, Savonarola, Coutarini, Pole, Occhino, and the superior souls near them to be the religious of that day; drawn to each other and under some cloud with the rest of the world, as the Methodists were in England, fifty years ago; or the Swedenborgians, or as the Transcendentalists were in Boston thirty years ago. They were the reformers, the abolitionists, the radicals of the hour, separated, to be sure, by their intellectual activity and culture from the masses who followed Luther and Savonarola, yet on their side in sympathy against the corruptions of Rome. Dumesnil calls Michel the conscience of Italy.

Arithmetic is a science of surfaces; probity, of essences. The most private self-searcher will be the most public and universal philosopher if his study is real. As the errors of the planets are periodical, and, when they have reached their maximum, are compensated by equal errors in the opposite direction; so the excesses of the mind in the direction of the understanding or analysis, are sure to be corrected by an equal addiction to synthesis.

We find the principles of the human constitution the same, when developed by philosophy, in all ages and nations. We find, after all its dissections, at bottom is an insatiable thirst for what they well denominate,—a state of mind being unable to stay, after its highest flights, till it arrive at a Being of unbounded greatness and worth. As a student of the laws of the mind, and habitually esteeming it wonderful in its functions and divine in its scope and potentiality, I am to be its apologist here also, and certainly do not sympathize with any objector who makes this majestic power responsible for the vices which the healthy intellect reprehends. We have all of us by nature a certain divination, presage, and parturient vaticination in our minds of some higher good and perfection than either power or knowledge. Knowledge is plainly to be preferred before power, as being that which guides and directs its blind force and impetus:  but Aristotle declares, that the origin of reason is not reason, but something better.

Illimitable prospects can best apply euphrasy to the understanding. Religion, that home of genius, will strengthen the mind as it does the character. The obedience to a man's genius is the particular of faith, and obedience to the moral laws the universal of faith. There is a probity of the Intellect, which demands virtues more costly than any Bible has enjoined. It consists in an absolute devotion to truth, founded in a faith in truth.

It was a wild poem of the Hindoos, yet profoundly true in its meaning, which described Love and Pity as two angels passing over Hell and witnessing the torments of souls. The tear dropped by Pity extinguished the fires. Another legend runs, that a divine messenger went to the world of pain. Being overcome at the sight of the tortures of the damned, he went through the horrible place, uttering everywhere "the five-lettered formula," which was caught up and repeated by the lost souls, and all were, by its repetition, delivered from their sufferings and translated into Swerga or Paradise.

"See within thee is the fountain of life, which flows ever and ever, if thou wilt only give it leave." A devout sentiment spoken in society has the effect of genius. Every principle is a war note. It will always be so. Whoever attempts to carry out the rule of right and love and freedom must take his life in his hand. I assure myself always of needed help, and go to the grave undaunted because I go not to the grave.

When we simply listen to this voice in our solitude, we know absurdly that it speaks the same sense to every man. We know beforehand that yonder man, whatever he says, must at last think as we do. Has he not two hands, two feet, hair on his head, lives by food, bleeds, laughs, cries, hopes and suffers? His dissent from me is all affectation. In my good hours I understand their goodness, and by my temptations I understand theirs. People can't get away from their brain, nor from their affection.

The advocate of the good cause finds a wealth of arguments and illustrations on his way. He stands for truth, and Truth and Nature help him unexpectedly and irresistibly at every step. All the felicities of example, of imagery, of admirable poetry, old religion, new thought, the analogies of science, throng to him, and strengthen his position. Nay, when we had to praise our own martyr, John Brown of Ossawotomie, I remember what a multitude of fine verses of old poetry fitted him exactly, and appeared to have been written for the occasion,—Milton and Herbert, Chapman and Beaumont, Wordsworth and Tennyson,—each offered his best verses.

# About the Editors

~

Frederick (Rick) Spaulding received a BA in English from Harvard College and a M.Ed. from Loyola University. He taught elementary school for seven years and high school English in the Chicago Public schools for twenty-seven years. Currently he is an independent lecturer, author, and researcher. He has given over eighty lecturers in the Midwest and East Coast of the U.S.

Maurice York received a BA in literature and history from Bard College and a Masters degree in Library and Information Science from the University of Illinois. He has been writing and conducting research into American literature and history for over ten years. He is currently a librarian at North Carolina State University.

Printed in the United States
139615LV00003B/46/P